MW01277494

*For Robert —
A remarkable man
blessed by God —
Marilee*

Faith Refined

Holding on When Life is Falling Apart

Marilee Donivan

Marilee Donivan

SF
Simple Faith Books
Boise, Idaho

Published by
Simple Faith Books
13347 W. Tapatio Drive
Boise, ID 38713

Printed in the United States of America
2012 First edition

To my wonderful children,

Brian and Kathi.

I thank God for you, daily.

MARILEE DONIVAN is an author, artist, speaker, and certified biblical counselor for grief, family, and personal counseling. She also has written and illustrated children's picture books, featuring Kandu, the lively toucan associated with her business, "You Can Do It! ART," and has published *Beginning Watercolor Painting*, a full-color illustrated book of watercolor lessons for children and adults, with demonstration DVDs.

More can be seen on her websites at
www. youcandoitart.com, and
www. kandubooks.com.

i

Acknowledgments

My deepest thanks go to God and my Savior, Jesus Christ, for giving me inner peace and holding me together in every aspect of life's joys and trials.

Thank you, Tom, for filling my life with love and laughter. You have such a servant's heart.

Thanks also go to my children, Brian and his wife Teresa, and Kathi and her husband Joe. You are a joy to be with and have given me your presence, loyalty, hugs, and prayers to warm my heart on cold, scary days.

Heartfelt thanks to Etta, who is my Naomi. You were there for my first baby steps of faith and have accompanied me at every turn on the journey. You are my role model for relationships and unwavering faith.

Thank you, Jim Tharp, for being my teacher of intercessory prayer, prayer partner through my darkest times, and dear friend. I marvel at God's goodness to have brought you into my family's life. Your inspirational influence and friendship is felt by us every day.

Thank you, Dr. Rob and Pam McCauley and Gregg and Sallee Middlekauff. You provided godly hospitality, comfort, and encouragement during our many visits to University of Utah Heart Transplant Unit.

Thank you, Brad and Marcia Gauss, for discipling Pat and me through your love of God's Word and authentic faith walk. You are treasured friends.

Thanks to the many, many prayer warriors and friends who have joined me in spiritual battles and prayed, believing God for great and wonderful things: Tim and Loraine Donivan, Dennis and Barbara Donivan, Mike and Anita Donivan, Shannon Donivan-Johns, Jerry Summers, Ed Schmitt, Teresa Schmitt, Molly and Gary Scollard, Marilyn and Fred Williams, Ralph and Sandy Turner, Ron and Barbara Clapp, Tim and Melodee Bunn, Volney Johnson, Ed Weaver, Michelle Miles, Pat Kuper, Doris and Bruce Yergenson, Mary and Nick Benzschawel, Sue Morrison, Christy Millington, Steve Ryan, Randy Basabe, Judy Rasmussen, Barbara Cobb, Mary Mitchell, Eve Ellis, Nancy Swanson, Tom and Donna Swanson, Brenda McNamara, Linda Schellenger, and Ruth Knoblock; and to Pat Donivan and Ann Swan who even now are enjoying their reward in heaven. You are each a part of this book because of your investment in prayer and in the strengthening of my faith. You are treasures in my heart and in the kingdom of God. May God pour richly into your lives to keep you filled up and overflowing!

Contents

Preface: "How Do You Get Faith Like That?"

"How do you get faith like that?" I asked. I was 21 years old. I was on my way to see my Marine Corps husband Pat who was training as a combat engineer officer at Camp Lejeune in preparation for deployment to Vietnam. My traveling companion was Donna, a friendly young woman I had met just a month earlier through base housing at Quantico, Virginia. Her husband Dick was also at Camp Lejeune. Donna and I were excited about the time we were going to spend with our husbands after a month-long separation from them.

The driving time was five and a half hours. We left home as early as we could on Friday, knowing the short winter days would require us to cover most of the miles in the dark. Donna and I chatted and laughed, enjoying the chance to get to know each other. November snowflakes began to fall, and as the wiper blades swished away the wet whiteness to clear our vision, our conversation turned to deeper subjects.

Donna told me about her faith and answered prayers. Her stories intrigued me. She spoke of Jesus Christ in a comfortable, familiar way, referring to Him simply as "Jesus."

I had never known anyone who talked about Jesus Christ as if He were a best friend. But that was exactly the impression she gave me—she included Him in everything she thought about and did.

My only association with Jesus Christ had been my upbringing in a church where God, Jesus Christ, and the Holy Spirit were referred to in written prayers, hymns, and sermons. But I had never heard anyone speak about "Jesus" as if they knew Him personally. I thought how wonderful it would be to have that kind of friendship with God.

I reminisced to Donna about the beautiful stained-glass windows in various churches my father had taken our family to. His career in the Marine Corps had moved us from coast to coast, to Hawaii, and overseas. Open doors throughout Europe had given us opportunity to soak in the elaborate architecture and inspiring art that fills chapels and cathedrals in Italy, France, and Germany.

I described how quiet places of reverence always had been like a magnet to me. As a young girl I would climb neighborhood church steps and slip inside to "visit God." I was pretty sure God would be there. I would sit alone in a carved wooden pew, enjoying the dark shadows interrupted by sunbeams sliding through the colored windows. The silence might be broken occasionally by echoes of footsteps that joined me for a few minutes during my reverie. "I don't remember how I talked to God," I confessed. "Maybe I recited some of the memorized psalms or liturgy I had been taught. I just remember reveling in the quietness, thinking, this is so beautiful and peaceful, God must surely be here."

Donna's experiences were very different from these, she said. She described her background. She had not traveled to the same places I had, but felt God's presence with her everywhere she went. All the time. With everything she did. I loved the idea of that. That was when I asked the question, "How do you get faith like that?"

There was a thoughtful silence. Then she said, "I guess by wanting it." There was more silence as I puzzled over her answer. I certainly wanted it, but I knew I didn't have it. I felt disappointed. Perhaps Donna misinterpreted my silence as a lack of further interest. For whatever reason, the conversation was diverted to other topics.

But God hears our unspoken thoughts. He knows the longing in our hearts. He was directing my feet on a path to "get faith like that."

A pivotal moment came several months later, the day I took Pat to the airport and tearfully said goodbye as he left for Vietnam. I came home, weeping. Stepping inside the one-bedroom apartment we had rented, I stood disconsolately, thinking the thirteen months he would be gone was a very long time. Out loud, I said, "God, this is the year I want to get to know You. Will You please come into my apartment and share it with me this year and let me get to know You?" For a moment I stood still, not expecting to hear a voice but wondering if God had heard my request. I sighed, took off my coat, and attended to other things, wondering what the year ahead might hold relative to my odd request.

Not long afterward, I was invited by Etta, Pat's mother, to go to a Billy Graham Crusade with her. There I heard the gospel message. Dr. Graham taught from the story of Adam and Eve in the garden. He told how God had given Adam and Eve everything they needed with only one negative instruction, "Don't eat from the tree of knowledge of good and evil."[1] The story in Genesis describes the temptation Satan brought for Eve to disobey God.[2] Eve succumbed and gave the fruit to Adam who also disobeyed God by eating it. The Bible describes this act as the first sin—a rebellious act against God's clear instructions. That same propensity for sin and rebellion, the Bible says, was passed on to every person since then and keeps us separated from God.[3]

Then I heard about Jesus, the perfect and only Son of God; how He took on human form and lived a perfect, sinless life.[4] He was Emmanuel, "God with us."[5] Jesus willingly took upon himself the punishment for all the sins of the whole world—people of every nation—in order to save us from eternally suffering what we deserve for our sins and rebellion.[6]

He offered Himself as our substitute, allowing Himself to be nailed to the cross, receiving punishment for offenses which weren't His.[7] This act of amazing love paid the penalty for all sin;[8] and God receives us back from our alienation from Him[9] when we humble ourselves, confess our sins, and accept His Son's death in the place of our own. It is a love-gift from God. His plan. His way. Accepting His way brings reconciliation with God for abundant life here on earth and eternal life in heaven.[10]

I was completely attentive to the message, which followed testimonies from people who had accepted this gift of forgiveness from God. They had described peace and a sense of new life and meaningfulness when they received Jesus Christ as their personal savior. A huge banner in the stadium proclaimed, "Jesus said, I am the Way, the Truth and the Life."[11] I pondered that statement, focusing on each word. I desperately wanted to know God in a close relationship if that were really possible. Was Jesus *the* Way? He said He was the Truth. Not, *a* truth. *The* Truth.

Then Billy Graham said, "Come, and give your heart to Jesus. The Bible says that if you have faith the size of a grain of mustard seed,[12] that is enough." I thought, *That is really all I have—faith like a tiny mustard seed. I know I don't understand all of this like I wish I did. But if this is God's way, I don't want to turn it down.* Driven by my longing to know

God, I accepted the invitation to believe and to come to Him through His Son, Jesus Christ. My heart pounded and tears cascaded down my cheeks as I walked down the steps of the stadium to make a statement of my faith. The little mustard seed took root. Relief and joy flooded my emotions.

The answer to the question, "How do you get faith like that?" was more than just wanting it. It was, also, making a conscious decision to ask God for that relationship with Him. To ask Him to forgive my sins. To accept His gift of forgiveness through His Son Jesus Christ. To submit my heart and my life to Him. To desire to live under His loving guidance, following Jesus.

Those first baby steps of mustard seed faith repurposed my journey through life. Days became infused with greater meaning, inner peace, and best of all, a solid sense of the nearness of God.

I invite you to join me on this faith journey. There will be many happy stops along the way filled with wonders, joys, and celebrations. Like other journeys, there also will be trials, trip-ups, fix-ups, and rest stops to catch our breath after break-downs and necessary repairs. Your faith journey—and mine—is worth the trip; it has many rewards and takes us to a destination we will enjoy forever.[13]

Chapter 1

Stretched Faith

"Bungee jumping?"

I met Tom through eHarmony.com. When I saw his written profile on my "Matches" page, I was intrigued. His statements of faith warmed my heart. His refreshing sense of humor made me grin. But, *bungee jumping?* Uh-oh. I ran it by my 32-year old daughter. "He sounds exciting," I broached.

"Uh, Mom, maybe he's a little too exciting for you."

My heart sank a little when she verbalized my secret suspicion. Nevertheless, Tom and I continued the eHarmony communication process, with cautious anticipation. Daily emails after some weeks became daily phone calls, and then both. With 600 miles between our homes, we continued to get to know each other without meeting face to face. Finally, after three months of descriptive letters, animated conversations late into the night, and meaningful prayers over the phone, we agreed it would be a good thing to meet in person.

Tom in person was exactly the way he had portrayed himself in our emails and phone calls. He is a communicator, enjoys telling stories, and is inquisitive with a keen listening ear—all skills he honed during the years he worked as an investigative journalist. He thrives on meeting new people, whether in a grocery store checkout line, at a ball game, or a neighborhood block party. He has a quick and quirky humor that puts people at ease and takes the ouch out of an awkward moment. Someone once said Tom could make a million dollars by manning a booth with a sign, "I'll be your friend for a dollar." He loves to help people and makes himself available to others. He is creative in business endeavors and social events, and makes the most of every involvement.

Best of all is the deep faith Tom has in Jesus Christ that is his foundation for relationships, decisions, and actions. After making numerous trips back and forth between our Idaho and Colorado homes, we agreed we believed it to be a God-ordained relationship, and sealed it with our vows to one another later that year.

It almost didn't happen. In any growing relationship there are hurdles. I sprang over Hurdle Number One—he didn't require a bungee-jumping wife. But on three different telephone calls, he fell asleep in the middle of our conversation. "Tom? TOM?" Are you THERE?" I found myself shouting into the telephone. No answer. While I was wondering whether I should call 911, or if I had just been stood up, he realized he had dozed off, and resumed the conversation with only a few peculiar gaps from the portion he had missed.

Am I that boring to him? I wondered, acutely aware that in the category of Adrenalin Rush my lifestyle had been at the opposite end of the spectrum from his. It turned out he was working long, hard hours, and was just worn out by midnight. He explained this and apologized. Relieved, I clambered over Hurdle Number Two.

Hurdle Number Three was of an entirely different nature. It came unexpectedly in the middle of a pleasant long-distance conversation we were having about faith and trust in God. Suddenly, Tom said, "I'm going to stretch your faith."

I took a deep breath. "You're going to stretch my faith?" I asked, working to keep an even tone of voice while my brow furrowed. Maybe this was going to be the deal-breaker for us. I was glad he couldn't see my disapproving frown. I hoped he would have some inspiring or funny explanation that would take the edge off my resistance.

"What are you talking about?" I asked carefully.

Tom answered slowly, sounding a little puzzled, "I don't know, exactly. I just know I'm going to stretch your faith."

I felt unsettled by his flat statement. *Who do you think you are?* I silently challenged during the lingering pause. A host of objections thundered through my mind as I reviewed the tumultuous events of the past eleven years, and the stretches of faith they had already produced. Four deaths in six months— the deaths of my best friend, my father, my grandmother, and my beloved husband of twenty-nine years; an emotional, stressful mission trip to Ukraine; the annulment of a one-year marriage to a fraudulent felon; and a season of depression while coming to terms with it all. I didn't want any more stretching. I continued my imaginary argument, *Hmph. Only God is the stretcher of my faith. You're not going to stretch my faith.*

It turned out we were both right. I skirted Hurdle Number Three for the time being, choosing to walk around it. But I would face it again, and ignoring it would not be an option.

Chapter 2

Hurdle Number Three

Someone once told me I was reasonably normal. *"Reasonably Normal?"* What does that mean? Does it mean I'm also Reasonably *Ab*normal? Or is it that I'm Almost Normal—but don't worry, with a little work, I might become Normal? Or is it just code communication for Boring? Although it first felt like an insult, it then struck my funny bone and I memorialized it on a normal white T-shirt in nice, reasonably normal letters. The T-shirt reads simply, "I'm Reasonably Normal." It always makes me laugh when I'm feeling down and puts things into perspective once again.

We each have our personal definition of normal, which can differ markedly from one person to the next. I think normal is whatever we make it—what we expect life to be at a given moment, day, or season. We usually work to maintain that normal. It gives us a sense of control, an ability to live with certain expectations. When our Personal Normal is interrupted, it can be very unnerving, sometimes even paralyzing, before we adjust to the new reality.

For me, it was a normal winter day in February. Snow lay like a comforting blanket outside our home while, inside, I cozied up with a soft sweater and aromatic coffee. It had been a productive morning. I grabbed a quick lunch so I could get back to work on the computer to tweak my business website. Tom was working in the office across the hall, creating marketing materials and advertising copy to help me in my home business enterprise. Tom is a give-it-all-you've-got kind of guy, and had spent some time on a particularly clever design. I heard him sigh with satisfaction and push back his chair. A moment later, he poked his head around the corner and congratulated himself.

"I did it! Now I need a break. I'm gonna exercise and stretch this old bod."

"Old Bod" was not what others thought when they met Tom. He was a very fit sixty years, with muscular arms and legs shaped by diligent exercise ever since his athletic days of competition. He thrived on physical activity and had pursued it over the years through football, fast-pitch softball, treadmill, gym workouts, outdoor bicycling, skiing, and running. These activities had intermissions of stretching, pushups, sit-ups and, as he often said, "huffin' and puffin'." Tom has an impish sense of humor, and easily quips a clever phrase at a moment's notice. I can count on a chuckle or two and a hearty laugh several times a day.

I heard him open the hall closet and pull out the elastic bands, knowing he was about to wrap them tightly around the doorknob, and begin his usual series of workouts, strengthening his arms, back, chest, and legs. I could hear him start his exercise routine while I typed away at the computer keyboard. The sounds of the bands vibrating against the closet door were louder than usual. "He certainly sounds energized today," I thought briefly, but my attention was focused on what I was writing. I vaguely wondered if he was taking out frustration with ferocity, or merely exercising with exuberance as I heard him pulling and releasing, and, yes, huffing and puffing, with extraordinary energy. A few minutes later it was quiet, and Tom appeared at the door of my office again, looking triumphant about his conquest over the elastic bands. He came over to my chair, bent low, and kissed me. "Did you think I was pulling the house down?" he chuckled with his irresistible grin.

Inwardly I reacted, *Yes, I sure did! What in the world were you doing!* But I just nodded and said, "Yeah, you really had a vigorous workout! You made quite a racket." I was totally engrossed with the display of my website on the computer screen and I was anxious not to be distracted from my train of thought. Tom recognized my riveted attention. He gave me a cheerful grin, another kiss, and disappeared around the corner. I went back to reorganizing photos on the webpage and deciding what the best captions would be for them.

Within a minute or two, I heard Tom snoring loudly in the next room. In the four years I had known Tom, I had seen him work hard, play hard, and have the enviable ability to sleep hard. For those of us who hit the pillow, then stare into the dark trying desperately to slow down the rush-hour traffic in our brains, it seems grossly unfair to lie next to someone who says goodnight and is immediately "out" for eight hours of uninterrupted sleep.

Hearing the snoring, I blinked in astonishment, thinking he really must have worn himself out with his exercise routine. I imagined that he had gone back into the other room to do his usual set of 200 push-ups and sit-ups, but had decided instead to just lie down and take a catnap.

His snoring was very loud. I stopped typing, thinking, "Wow, it's amazing how he can fall asleep like that." I typed another sentence. The snoring was incredibly loud, very unusual. I felt uneasy. I left my chair and went into the living room. I saw Tom lying face down on the carpet in a position that suggested he had done a few push-ups before falling asleep. But something wasn't right.

"TOM!" I called, as I approached him, "TOM, are you all right?" Then I saw he wasn't. His eyes were open, but staring and vacant.

"Tom, WAKE UP! Please, TOM, WAKE UP!"

His body was in a full stretched-out position on the rug. His arms were bent at the elbows, hands by his shoulders. His head was turned slightly toward the floor, and to his right. He looked as if he had been doing push-ups. It had only been a minute since he had kissed me. But he was not responding. Deep guttural sounds rattled loudly from his throat. Alarm bells clanged throughout my whole body. I knew I had to do something immediately.

My mind ricocheted back thirteen years, when I had been at the same crisis point with my husband Pat. At age 48, Pat had been diagnosed in 1993 with an enlarged heart. Tests revealed his heart had a 20% ejection fraction, ominously below the normal range of 60-75%. The concerned doctor insisted on admitting him to the hospital for monitoring, which led to a stay of several days while other tests were run. The doctor refused to discharge him until I learned how to deliver CPR. A nurse trained me in an empty hospital room. It turned out I used the training. Pat's weakened heart stopped two years later while he was sitting in the living room, talking on the telephone. It was obvious that the

CPR training had not been just a good, theoretical idea, but a very practical provision for the event the doctors knew was inevitable.

On that awful occasion years ago, Pat's mother, Etta, was sitting with us in the living room as he chatted sociably on the phone with Barbara, his sister-in-law, swapping ideas about fishing and cooking. His heart quietly gave up and the conversation stopped mid-sentence. His mother and I pulled Pat to the floor in order to begin CPR. Etta called 911 while I began vigorous chest compressions and oxygen-delivering breaths as I had been taught. It seemed like a very long time before the ambulance and EMTs arrived, but it may have been only ten minutes. I was physically exhausted when they burst through the door and took over providing air and chest compressions. Etta and I had retreated to a distant view from across the room to stay out of their way, and prayed as they swept him out to the ambulance for the short trip to our small town's hospital. We hurried to the car and followed the flashing lights and siren in the dark, praying aloud as we sped behind the ambulance.

Pat's weakened heart had worn out over the two-year period of waiting for a heart transplant, and his heart was not strong enough to be restored to function, in spite of the skilled EMTs and hospital personnel using defibrillation shock therapy and every resource available.

With this vivid memory reverberating, I stared in disbelief at my beloved Tom on the living room floor and realized every minute was precious. I was in emotional shock, from the all too familiar scene; but mentally I was on full alert, knowing Tom had to have immediate oxygen and his heart needed to pump oxygen to his brain and other organs. I couldn't feel a pulse. I would need to roll him over on his back so that I could begin CPR. Kneeling beside him, I frantically pulled on his broad shoulders to try to get him onto his back. He was too heavy. Tom's six-foot structure weighed about 205 pounds. There was no one to help me. There wasn't room to get to the other side and push him over because he was wedged against the couch. I was agonizing over the seconds that were slipping by. I wasn't strong enough, I realized with horrifying dismay.

Suddenly, I remembered the First Aid course I had taken decades earlier as a Girl Scout. An unconscious victim may be rolled over by crossing the legs and pulling on the feet to roll the body. It had been very successful with my twelve-year-old Girl Scout friends. In a burst of hope, I scrambled on my knees towards Tom's limp feet, crossed them, and pulled with all my strength. Tom's solid frame didn't budge. Disbelief and despair joined forces in my pounding heart. I felt utterly helpless to do what I knew had to be done.

Muscle weakness produced a fiery burning down my back, through the backs of my legs, and into my feet. How could I continue? I cried aloud, "Lord, I can't roll him over! Please help me! Please! Help me roll him over!" Then I realized his bent right arm was creating an obstacle that was preventing his body from turning. I straightened his right arm against his side, and pulled with all my might and determination, desperate for his body to roll. "Lord, I need you! Please send an angel to help me! I can't do this!" Tears were sliding down my cheeks. I gave another mighty attempt, lifting and pulling his left shoulder toward me again with all the strength I could muster. And his body rolled over.

I tilted his head back to clear the airway, pinched his nose shut, took a full breath, covered his mouth with mine, and blew into his mouth. 911! I had to call 911! How could I not have thought of this first? My heart sank as I realized I had to leave Tom's side in order to call for help. I gave some more chest compressions and stumbled to the kitchen to get the cordless phone. I dialed 911 and put the phone on speaker function as I staggered back to Tom's side, gave him another breath, and resumed chest compressions. The emergency dispatcher answered. I could hear the near panic and strident pitch in my voice as my sentences ran together.

"My husband is unconscious, he has stopped breathing, there is no pulse, I need to give CPR."

The dispatcher expertly took over with his training: "Don't hang up. We're sending someone. Find the center of his chest. Put the heel of your left hand on his chest. Put your other hand on top of your left hand. Get right over his chest. Keep your elbows straight, and give 300 firm compressions straight down. Compress the chest at least two inches. Start now!"

While I was pumping hard on Tom's chest, I thought the dispatcher had forgotten something. He had said nothing about breathing. I shouted at the handset on the floor next to me, "Shouldn't I breathe for him?" All this time, I was breathing hard, myself, and performing the compressions vigorously.

"No, just do the compressions. Do three hundred of them!"

This was different from my hospital training fifteen years earlier, and I was skeptical, but I followed his directions and concentrated on the chest compressions. Later, I learned that the most recent recommendation from the American Heart Association was indeed to forego the breathing when one is the sole resuscitator. It is best to keep the blood moving through the heart and into the organs, especially to the brain. The blood will carry the residual oxygen that is already in the body. Keeping the heart "pumping" with forceful external pressure is imperative. If there is more than one rescuer to perform CPR, one can do the breathing, and the other can do the chest compressions. But with just one person, it has been found that letting up on the chest compressions in order to deliver air allows opportunity for blood to backflow into the heart. This can cause secondary and life-threatening results.

I didn't know any this information at the time, so I was puzzled and worried. But I followed the instructions. One does this when a steady voice of authority speaks as clearly and confidently as this dispatcher did. It is an indescribable relief and comfort to hear calm instructions during times of panic and distress. I followed his directions with the telephone handset at my side. At the same time, I was giving information, my address, and the directions to my home.

The dispatcher interrupted, "We'll find it! The ambulance is on its way."

My legs were trembling from the exertion of their unfamiliar position tucked under me as I knelt beside Tom and continued the compressions. Tom's color was gray, and I knew his life could be gone forever. The snoring sounds had ceased. I learned later these are called agonal gasps, and are a common occurrence prior to death.

My back and legs ached and throbbed. I prayed God would give me strength, not knowing how long I would be able to persist. The pain was excruciating, but heart-wrenching fear created adrenalin to continue. A provision from God. I suddenly remembered with dismay that the front door was locked. I had to leave Tom again to get the door open for the help that was coming. Hurrying back, I resumed CPR, worrying about how much damage had occurred during the two times I had to stop CPR for these necessary tasks.

It may have been only two or three minutes later that help arrived, rushing through the front door, calling out,

"Paramedics!" I was relieved and surprised at how quickly they arrived. I had expected a longer duration, based on my experience years earlier. A team of four focused men and one woman swiftly took over as I struggled on my knees to get out of their way. It was a dreadfully familiar scene.

It was a team of advanced EMTs. They found him asystole, without any heartbeat. The paramedics cut off Tom's shirt and used a portable AED to send a shock to his heart. His heart took the jolt, and restarted with an inefficient heart rhythm. He did not regain consciousness. The team fitted him with a neck collar to immobilize his head, pumped oxygen through a bag valve mask because his breathing had not resumed, and injected drugs used for cardiac arrest victims.

Meanwhile a member of the team took me to the kitchen to ask me questions about how long Tom had been down before they arrived, and about his medical background, which I filled in as best I could. As far as I knew, Tom had had no previous heart problems or any other serious illness or hospitalization. He was on no medications. He seemingly had been very healthy until this catastrophe.

Monitoring his heart and providing oxygen, they lifted him onto a stretcher. As I anxiously watched Tom being wheeled out the door and lifted into the ambulance, the paramedic finished gathering information from me and told me where they were taking him. With sirens blaring, the vehicle sped to a local branch of St. Luke's Hospital about four miles away.

By this time, two neighbors were standing at the open front door. They had seen the emergency vehicles and rushed over, worried and anxious to help. I motioned to them to come in, and told them what was happening in a few abbreviated sentences. Connie insisted on driving me to the hospital, not trusting me to safely drive myself. I felt in control and believed I would be fine, grimly remembering I had done this successfully once before, thirteen years earlier, but I was touched by her loving insistence under such dire circumstances. I had felt so very, very alone next to Tom in his extreme need, and I accepted her offer with gratitude.

When we arrived at the emergency admissions desk, I had to give more information to the clerk, all the time frantically wondering what was happening behind the closed doors to the emergency room that held Tom. I was told to take a seat and someone would come get me.

Connie and Jan waited with me during the anxious time that decisions were being made about what to do for Tom and where he needed to be. These two calm women were a great comfort, friends willing to be with me, sharing my hope for some good news.

God is wonderful in the way He gives a calm and inner peace when our eyes and ears tell us the whole world is falling apart. In His goodness, He sends friends, neighbors, and even strangers. Through their compassion and giving, God provides emotional and practical support. Connie's husband John joined Connie, Jan, and me at the hospital as soon as he could. Connie and John are special neighbors. We had connected instantly when we met on our moving day two years earlier. We moved in next door to one another on the very same day, and helped each other carry things into our homes. We had laughed a lot, commiserated a little, and swapped anecdotes freely, developing a mutual appreciation and genuine love for each other's family. Their presence provided a sense of real-world connection and stability that I needed during this déjà vu nightmare.

The Emergency Room doctor's unhesitating decision was to send Tom immediately by ambulance from the branch hospital's emergency room to the main hospital's Coronary Care Unit in downtown Boise because it was better equipped to manage critical care. The doctor told me Tom had experienced sudden cardiac arrest and was in critical condition. Cardiac arrest is a complete and sudden cessation of the heart's function, with no early symptoms or warning. He did not tell me that over 90% of the time it is fatal, particularly in a case like Tom's when the patient remains unresponsive following emergency medical intervention.

John and Connie took me to the larger hospital in their car, with Jan following. Downtown in the waiting room of the

Coronary Care Unit, Dr. Souza visited with me. He explained that the degree of brain injury for patients surviving cardiac arrest depends on the length of time the brain is without oxygen while the patient is "down." He asked how long Tom was down (meaning without aid of CPR). I wasn't sure exactly how long he had been down before I saw him, or how many minutes had passed while I struggled to get him rolled over, started CPR, then had to leave his side in order to call 911, began CPR again, then had to leave him again to unlock the front door, and finally resumed CPR until the EMTs arrived.

I told him I thought the whole event had totaled no longer than five minutes before the ambulance arrived, but it's difficult to judge the passing of time in crisis moments. I estimated that I had given Tom uninterrupted CPR for two to three minutes, and that perhaps it had been five minutes from the time I called 911 before the EMT's took over.

The doctor looked surprised and pleased that he could give me a glimmer of hope. He said, "If it was only five minutes or less, his chance of coming through is improved. With each additional minute, the chances lessen. Only 5 to 10 percent of patients who suffer cardiac arrest outside a hospital survive." He went on to caution me with more sobering information. "For survivors, there are after-effects with brain injury likely. The extent of brain injury has to do with how much time the brain was without oxygen." He would not make any predictions, but went on to tell me the emergency procedures the hospital was providing.

He explained hypothermia protocol, saying it is a new technique of rapidly cooling the patient that some hospitals have begun to use, and is believed to protect brain function among patients who are without oxygen for a period of time, such as victims of cardiac arrest. He said they had begun the cooling process on Tom's comatose body. If he survived, they hoped the hypothermia would have preserved adequate brain function. It was clear that there were many unanswered questions and there would be a time of waiting before I could know any additional information.

At the time, St Luke's Hospital was one of a small number of hospitals in the U.S. that had adopted the practice of using induced hypothermia for cardiac arrest patients. The application of cooling blankets and ice around the body was still being evaluated in the medical field. Findings were that patients receiving the hypothermia therapy had survived with better results than those who survived without the hypothermia application. Recent medical literature suggests that cooling helps protect the brain by slowing metabolism and reducing the brain's need for oxygen and nutrients. The procedure was experimentally initiated by doctors who recognized it mimics the environment of someone who has fallen through an icy pond, remained submerged for many minutes and is later slowly warmed and revived. Some such incidents have resulted in the hypothermic victim's resuscitation with preserved brain function, as compared with individuals at normal body temperature who had been without oxygen for the same length of time.

For this reason, Dr. Souza explained, St. Luke's Hospital had begun using the technique. Tom's body would be quickly cooled to about 33 degrees C (92 degrees F), and kept there for 24 hours. At the same time, Tom had been given injections to sedate and paralyze his body to prevent shivering. Shivering is the body's built-in mechanism to warm itself, something that would be counterproductive to the intended cooling process. He repeated what I had heard earlier, that Tom was "critically ill and unstable," medical terminology which means a condition which cannot survive without life support. He was in acute respiratory failure and at significant risk for degeneration of brain function, in this case caused by decreased oxygen in the blood and decreased rate of blood flow.

Dr. Souza said it would be a "wait and see" time, but that I could see Tom, and then should consider going home to get some rest because it was going to be "a long road ahead." I didn't ask what that long road might look like. I decided I had enough to deal with for now. I explained that Tom's son was living in Colorado, 600 miles away, and asked if I should tell him to come to Boise. The doctor said, "No, not at this time, it isn't necessary." This gave me hope for Tom's recovery prospects. It was about 9:30 P.M.

I did call Steven, Tom's seventeen-year-old son, to tell him his father had collapsed, his heart had stopped, the ambulance had taken him to the hospital, and he was in the CCU in a coma, but receiving excellent care. I added that the prognosis was uncertain. Steven is a quiet, reserved young man. I couldn't see his face. I wished so much I could read his facial expression and body language. I didn't know if he fully understood the gravity of his father's condition. I actually didn't know enough at the time to draw my own conclusions. So I told Steven I would call him again as soon as I had more information. I spoke a prayer with Steven and hung up, aching for Steven's emotions, which I could only imagine. Remembering my own children's anguish in their similar situation years earlier, I desperately wished I could be with Steven at this uncertain time to comfort and pray with him.

A nurse came into the waiting room and said she would show me to Tom's room. Outside the CCU doors she showed me the telephone to request admittance and instructed me about hand washing once we were inside the door. She led me through the Coronary Care Unit. It was a large room with desks, telephones, cabinets, and computers in the center, surrounded by rooms of beds on the perimeter. Each room was a cubicle just large enough for a hospital bed, sink, one chair, and an impressive array of monitors and IV bag stands with tubing. Each cubicle's sliding glass door had a curtain that could be drawn for privacy and to block out some of the light from the nurses' work areas in the center.

Like several other rooms, Tom's room was uncurtained, open for full view to allow vigilant observation by his nurse sitting on a stool at a tall table outside the glass door. Her attention was riveted on Tom and the surrounding paraphernalia. Monitors recorded levels of blood pressure, heart rate, oxygen, glucose, life-sustaining drugs, and respiratory mechanisms.

The watchful nurse looked down only to make written notes regarding the undulating green lines and constantly changing numbers on the black monitor screens. Frequently she left her chair, came into the room, and adjusted the flow from one or more of the IVs that were attached to Tom's body. There were IV tubes all up and down his arms. He still wore the neck collar that immobilized his head. This was protocol, I was told, for patients who fall to the floor unwitnessed. I couldn't say for sure he had avoided a neck injury because I hadn't witnessed his collapse. So Tom was consigned to the neck brace as a precaution.

An endotracheal tube extended from a mouthpiece down his esophagus, and the respirator whooshed rhythmically in the room, forcing air into his lungs. His color was gray, and he lay with his eyes closed, while the external medical apparatus worked to sustain life. Chemicals seeped through the IVs into his still body. I wondered when his eyes had closed. I didn't think to ask. It was an unnerving sight to see this vibrant, strong man in this foreign environment.

I spoke to the nurse and she explained the reasons and functions of the numerous tubes and measurements. She was knowledgeable, confident, and compassionate. Although it was late, past visiting hours, she invited me to stay by Tom's bed as long as I wanted to. There was no way to hold his hand. IVs were taped to the backs of them, and his hands were wrapped and tied to the side rails of the bed so that if he regained consciousness he wouldn't pull at the breathing tube as half-conscious patients will try to do. I stood next to his bed for a long time, praying, asking God to comfort him, guard him, and be very close to him in his unconscious state.

I was struggling to absorb and accept the reality of the scene. Sudden crises produce these "other world" kinds of sensations. Emotions react to sudden trauma and drastic changes before the mind can wrap itself around the facts and reason its way through them. This is part of being in emotional shock and acts as a kind of protection. It is a merciful cushion to help absorb the full brunt of a collision of calamities against our regulated routines.

Tom was in very critical condition. The nurse checked his

pupils with a pinpoint flashlight in the dark room. I could see from my position next to her that they were dilated and had no reaction to the light. The measurement was seven millimeters. This was not a sign for a good outcome. Unreactive pupils in both eyes in patients admitted to the hospital is a powerful predictor of death, regardless of treatment given. Traditionally, both pupil diameter and reaction to light have been examined to confirm the diagnosis of death. I remembered Dr. Souza's words and knew there were some rougher waters ahead, so, dodging medical paraphernalia, I spoke into Tom's ear, "I love you, Tom. I love you," fearing they would be the last words he would hear from me.

When I returned to the CCU waiting room, John told me Connie and Jan had gone downstairs to the hospital cafeteria to find me something to eat. I was surprised when I looked at my watch; it was almost 10:00 P.M. I appreciated their unsolicited kindness and felt fortified as I ate a bit of the turkey and mashed potatoes they brought back. My sweet-spirited neighbors waited patiently, conversed softly until I was ready to leave, then drove me home. I marveled at their graciousness and love and felt completely inadequate as I tried to express my thanks. At such times we just hope someone can read our grateful hearts. In the darkness of the late hour, we exchanged words of hope and faith, then said goodnight. They said they would come to the hospital to be with me again the next day.

Once inside, I called my daughter, Kathi, to let her know what had happened. She and her husband Joe insisted she come over immediately and stay with me for the night. Their obvious compassion and concern touched my heart, and I gratefully accepted. Kathi called her brother in Colorado. Brian, his wife Teresa, and their 4-year old daughter Kelli left their home before daybreak to begin the twelve hour drive from Ridgway.

Kathi lived only a mile from my home, and she was at my door within fifteen minutes. We hugged, and briefly discussed possible plans, realizing things were entirely unpredictable. We decided the best thing would be to go to bed and try to get some sleep to prepare for the uncertainty of the next day.

As I brushed my teeth, I marveled at the mundane things that go on in the midst of a crisis. Brushed teeth, for example. Going through the motions, feeling like it must be someone else in this situation. *Not I. Not again. Couldn't be.* I thought, *This must be what sleep-walking is like.* Moving around the house, taking care of things like locking doors and turning off lights, making sure the phone was close at hand in case of a call from the hospital. Functioning, but feeling numb, I was surprised I could even think of these routine tasks. I felt as if I were on autopilot.

Kathi and I said goodnight to one another and agreed we wouldn't plan for a specific time to wake up, knowing it probably would be early. We didn't guess just how early it would be.

Chapter 3

Tears in a Bottle

At 2:00 a.m. the telephone rang. The nurse was very business-like, saying, "You need to come to the hospital; the doctor wants to see you."

My heart was already pounding. I asked, "Is Tom alive?" There was a pause, lasting much too long, as my mind darted from one possible scenario to another, trying to prepare itself for her answer.

Alarmed, I needed to know, "Is Tom ALIVE?"

"Yes," she said, "But the doctor needs to talk to you." It was clear she wasn't going to give me any further information.

I awakened Kathi, and we were in the car within five minutes, heading across town, not talking, silently praying, realizing that a two o'clock in the morning conference is more than a casual appointment for a medical update.

Dr. David Sasso took us into a private consultation room in the CCU and quietly described the situation. "Tom is very, very sick. He is the sickest person here in the CCU. If even ONE..." (he paused to see if I understood his emphasis) "...of all those tubes were to be removed for just 30 seconds, he would be gone. He is critically ill and deteriorating. We don't know if he will make it. He could be gone in the next 24 hours. You need to let anyone who needs to see him know that they must come right away." The new urgency was alarming.

I called Steven in Grand Junction and explained his dad's declining condition. We discussed the best way for him to get to Boise. Neither Boise nor Grand Junction airports have many flights on a daily or night-time schedule. Steven wanted to leave immediately and drive straight through. I was fearful of his traveling on Colorado's icy roads in February and in the middle of the night and told him so. I was relieved when he agreed to wait until daylight to begin the trip. Kathi and I earnestly prayed Tom would make it through the night, but the medical picture was foreboding. I wondered if Steven would arrive in time, but all we could do was trust God, and lean on Him for this merciful provision. We prayed for Steven's physical and emotional safety as he traveled, concerned that he had so many miles to cover, but there was no more expedient way for him to come than by air.

I was drawn like a magnet to Tom's room. I wanted so much to see him, not knowing how many more hours or days I might be able to look at the face of the man I deeply loved. It was anguish to see him with such uncertainty wrapped around him, but it was more agonizing to be away from his side. The desire to be near him overcame my dreadful awareness of his weakening organs, probable brain damage, and impending death. So many unknowns. The best wisdom seemed to be to live the moment, pray it through, and trust God's peace-giving presence, knowing God is always in complete control even when we don't understand the whys and wherefores.

Kathi joined me at Tom's bedside. It was a sobering sight. Tom's face was gray and his eyes were slits in his unconscious state. Kathi was shocked at his appearance, and whispered her concern, "Is he alive?" I assured her he was, and pointed to the monitors as evidence. She was amazed, felt fairly certain he wouldn't last another 24 hours, and prepared herself for the doctor's warning to become reality. While I remained next to Tom, Kathi quietly stepped back and whispered to the nurse the looming question, "Do you ever see patients come out of a condition like this?"

The nurse murmured her answer, "Not usually."

Kathi went into the CCU waiting room with a pillow and blanket provided by the nurse, and lay down on a bench to get some sleep.

I stood by Tom's bed in the dim room with the surrounding beeps and green lights of the monitors. I whispered prayers for Tom, for me, for Steven, for the doctors and nurses, for the equipment, for wisdom and insight. For strength. I sat for a while in the lonely chair and recited memorized Bible verses that have sustained me through trials of many kinds. The nurse came in to read the instruments and make adjustments on the flow of chemicals through the IVs. My concentrated thoughts and prayers were interrupted, so I returned to the waiting room. Kathi was asleep on one of the benches. During the pre-dawn hours, I drifted between the CCU and the waiting room numerous times.

Later that morning, our church's pastor, Tim Bunn, came into the waiting area. He told us the church had already begun to pray for Tom. I had called Tim only a few hours earlier and was touched by his swift and compassionate response to my request for prayer. He asked if he could go into the CCU to pray for Tom and anoint him with oil. Of course! Kathi and I went with him. As Pastor Tim placed oil on Tom's forehead, reminding us of the Biblical symbol of the Holy Spirit, we three laid our hands on Tom's motionless body and asked God to supply strength and renewed functioning to bring Tom back to health. We prayed for God's protection and thanked Him for His goodness and sustaining power. We couldn't predict the outcome, but knew God was ever-present, loving, and all-powerful as He always is. This comforting truth sustained us.

Some new urgent developments challenged the expertise of the CCU professionals. Internal bleeding was filling Tom's abdominal cavity, causing his blood pressure to drop, further stressing his weakening body. An injured spleen was the origin of the bleeding. Intravenous fluids were quickly increased and he was given 6 units of blood and three units of packed red cells to replace blood that had left circulation and was filling the abdominal and chest cavity spaces surrounding the organs. Filling up these spaces put pressure on the lungs and decreased their ability to expand sufficiently for optimum oxygenation. I asked if anything was going to be done about the internal bleeding, but was told that Tom was too unstable even to be transported to Imaging to verify the suspected source of the bleeding. If surgery were necessary it would be out of the question, anyway, given his fragile condition.

I became aware that precarious shifts in the balance were occurring hourly, as doctors and nurses vigilantly evaluated the complicated interactions of heart, lungs, brain, circulation, respiration, kidneys, liver, and spleen. His pupils remained dilated and unresponsive, a sign of deep coma, indicating brain stem injury, and because that status had persisted beyond six hours, expectation of survival diminished to zero. This specific information wasn't given to me at the time; I learned it later. His kidneys were in oliganuric failure, he had respiratory failure, and his blood pressure was hypotensive at 60/35. He was in frank shock. The development of shock is associated with hypotension, which ultimately results in multi-organ system failure. Organs fail as the oxygen supply to them is decreased. This was the status of Tom's condition. Even with the mechanical respirator faithfully delivering oxygen to Tom's lungs, oxygen was not being carried by the blood in sufficient supply to his vital organs.

Hypothermia therapy had been used to protect the brain, but it contributed, with other factors, to decreased blood pressure, which reduced the circulatory system's ability to carry oxygen to all the body's vital organs. Tom's body decompensated; that is, it could not overcome the series of dangerous developments and was deteriorating in spite of the best procedures made available to him.

It was apparent the induced hypothermia had created a threatening situation due to the unique problems that were amassing themselves in the face of medical expertise. So the hypothermia therapy was stopped and Tom's body was rewarmed after twelve hours instead of the usual protocol of 24 hours. Blood lactate level continued to rapidly climb. Lactate levels over 2.0 are serious indicators of poor outcomes. Tom's had climbed to 15.8 within a time frame that represented yet another predictor of mortality. Dr. Sasso noted on Tom's record, "Patient is critically ill and deteriorating in the CCU."

With new challenges and swift changes in Tom's precarious condition, there were many obstacles to overcome, with obvious reasons to expect a poor outcome. As organs fail, there comes a kind of domino effect as the body has fewer reserves to draw upon. With each new organ failure, prospects of survival, already unlikely, dimmed further.

As I stood beside Tom's bed, thinking of the enormous struggles his body was encountering, the nurse quietly asked me if I wanted them to do everything needed to keep Tom alive. I was puzzled by the question, thinking, *Isn't this the Critical Care Unit? Isn't that what you do here?* I do not blame this dedicated young nurse for neglecting to clarify the significance of her question. It must be the most dreaded conversation any empathetic nurse or doctor will have with family members. She surely thought I would know the urgent need and meaning behind her question. But I didn't. All I knew is that I was praying, and Tom was still under watchful medical care in the CCU. The moment seemed more like a continuation of an unfolding story, one that I could not know or write the ending for. I could only wait.

With little experience in such things, and in the enormous emotional and spiritual challenge of the hour, I naïvely thought that if Tom were to die, it would be in spite of receiving all the intensive therapies in the CCU, and in spite of all the equipment and medical expertise. Not receiving further information from the nurse, I said, "Yes, of course I want you to do everything that needs to be done." I did not understand she was telling me that every medical strategy currently being used was not expected to help Tom recover, but would only perpetuate minimal functioning with mechanical life support. She made a note on his record. "FULL CODE." I had no idea that implied end of life artificial support for a dying patient.

There was a reason I missed the full significance of her question. My only other experience like this had been thirteen years earlier in another Emergency Room with another loved one. On that occasion, I was waiting anxiously after my husband Pat had been brought by ambulance to the hospital following his sudden cardiac arrest. After 45 minutes of aggressive medical procedures, the doctor approached me to say they had done everything they could do to revive him, but without success. She quietly explained the emergency interventions they had tried which had proven insufficient to resuscitate him. She described the present complications and futility of proceeding. Then, showing great compassion, she gently asked me, "Do you want us to keep trying?"

The doctor had maintained professional composure as she spoke, but I clearly sensed her deep sadness and disappointment that medical knowledge and training are ultimately limited by a multitude of uncontrollable variables, beyond man's intellect, skills, and education. No matter how much we know, how much we study, how much we achieve, some things will always be beyond our control. Because of her careful and definitive briefing, I fully understood the situation and sadly agreed they need not continue their efforts. They had done everything possible, and it was necessary that I accept this finality—a very different endpoint than my faith-filled expectations. It wasn't what I had believed would happen, but it was without ambiguity.

The scenario in the CCU with Tom didn't have that kind of clarity for me. It's odd how the brain and the emotions function under stress. It's a good reminder to put some things, the ones we can, on the back burner when the stress factor is high. In the case of Tom, I believe missing the implications of the nurse's question was God's way to keep me in harmony with His better plan and His perfect timing. Since I hadn't fully grasped the implications, I was quick to answer her; after all, it seemed an obvious and easy decision. I believed that the outcome was forthcoming, and that I just needed to be patient, trust God, and wait for whatever that outcome would be.

At the core of my response was the realization that all life is ultimately in the hands of God, and that He alone determines the number of our days according to His wisdom. I had wrestled with that issue when Pat died, and found peace that settled into my spirit regarding God's goodness and wisdom even in the darkest hours. God uses many things—even our weaknesses—as He works all things together for good. I am sure I have seen Him more clearly in times of uncertainty, weariness, inability, and fright, than I have during times of self-confidence and strength.

There is always the temptation to cast aside our faith when things don't look like they are working out as we think they should, or as we prayed. Just as Jesus was tempted by the devil in the wilderness in both physical and spiritual ways, we will be tempted in physical and spiritual ways, too. In times of great distress, I've been tempted to doubt God's nearness, to think He is unwilling to answer prayers, to believe He has no regard for my anguish, my tears, or my longings to be close to Him. These are lies the devil suggests to our minds when we are most vulnerable during experiences of woundedness and pain. At these times we need friends who will remind us of the truth. The truth is, God knows exactly what is going on in our broken hearts and He cares deeply. In the poetic language of the psalmist, He catches our tears in a bottle and notes them in a book.

"You number my wanderings; Put my tears into Your bottle; Are they not in Your book? When I cry out to You, Then my enemies will turn back; This I know, because God is for me" (Psalms 56:8-9).

To think He takes note of every hurt, even writes them down, and keeps the essence of them in His personal collection! Not only that, the reason He does it is because He is *for* us!

It was a Jewish custom of mourners to catch their tears in a bottle and present the bottle to demonstrate their shared grief. The bottles would be placed in the tomb of the loved one as a sign of their devotion. Since reading this many years ago, I've sometimes envisioned my tears being shed into a bottle, then corked to preserve them as precious evidence of the difficult reality of valleys I've walked. The pits I've fallen into. The failures. And the emotional caves I've retreated into when uncertain footing in trying times was almost overwhelming. It's not a bottle of self-pity. It's a declaration to God that even as I give Him my tears, my heart is still tied to His. *"Though He slay me, yet I will still trust Him"* (Job 13:15). He has proven His love to me dramatically, many times, and His love is worth far more to me than the tears I've shed.

David Wilkerson wrote in one of his World Challenge Pulpit Series notes about the sacrifices that are involved in desiring a deeper experience of faith and intimacy with God:

"Those who have a passion to draw closer to the Lord will have to endure more profound, mysterious, intense temptations in the spiritual realm—in the thought life, the faith life. There will be deep, dry times that try one's soul."

Our tears are precious to God. He knows the number of them, and keeps them tenderly in His care. They do not go unnoticed.

"Therefore, do not cast away your confidence, which has great reward. For you have need of endurance, so that after you have done the will of God, you may receive the promise" (Hebrews 10:35-36).

Chapter 4

Two Thumbs Up

As Day Two progressed, the essential pH levels in the human body became a focus of concern. Tom's body was losing its pH balance; frequent measurements showed increasing acidity. Acidosis occurs when there is insufficient oxygen getting to the tissues. Tom's low blood pressure wasn't moving blood efficiently, and a domino effect was occurring. The enormous challenge in critical care is the managing of complex relationships among all the body's systems. It can be a "Catch 22" effect; that is, while treating one system that is in critical condition, another system may be negatively affected, and an unavoidable progression leads to irreversible multi-organ failure.

There was no doubt that the prognosis was very grave. With Tom under expert and vigilant care, I returned home to try to get some badly needed sleep. Tom's son Steven had made it into Boise and called to say he would come to the hospital early the next morning.

Steven was in the CCU waiting room when I arrived at the hospital early Wednesday morning. He had already seen his father. I was so thankful Tom had made it through the night and that Steven would be able to check on him periodically during the day and talk to him even though he was still in a deep coma. There have been documentations of comatose patients who awakened later and reported they had heard conversations in their rooms. They could even repeat what had been said. Because a comatose person has no visible signs of being able to hear or see or respond neurologically, some people will discuss things in a patient's room they would not otherwise talk about. I determined to talk to Tom encouragingly, and to pray words of praise and faith, as if he were fully alert and could hear every word. I guarded my conversations with nurses and doctors so that before we talked about his failing internal systems, I requested we step outside the glass walls where he wouldn't hear our words.

I worried it would be difficult for Steven to see his father's helpless condition; it was frightening. I needn't have worried. During his hours of travel from Colorado, Steven had been given peace of mind and a calm expectation that his father would pull through in spite of the dire prognosis. He was not anxious; he was simply expecting and waiting for his father to get better. His inner assurance showed as he calmly stood beside Tom's bed, taking in the array of life-sustaining tubes, beeping monitors, and his father's still body and closed eyes, so unlike the man of vitality he had been just three days earlier. I was surprised at Steven's ability to view this scene with apparent composure.

There were serious indicators warning of further deterioration—rising creatinine and increasing troponin levels. His creatinine was at 3.1 and troponin level was 59.98. His abdomen was distended from the extensive internal bleeding, and anemia had developed. His continuing extremely low blood pressure and a partial lung collapse affected his breathing, further lowering oxygen levels in his tissues.

Throughout the day, wonderful friends came to spend time with me in the waiting room when I took a break away from Tom's side. They prayed, encouraged, and helped the time pass by talking about daily things going on in their families, bringing forth some welcome smiles and laughter. Our mirth probably puzzled some. Everyone in a CCU waiting room has serious circumstances front and center on their minds. But emotions can bear only so much heaviness at a time. Laughter is one of God's provisions, especially during times of great stress. Not only is it a physical release, relaxing the body, it also brings mental relief from whirling thoughts of doubt, worry, and fears. The funny stories and smiles uplifted my aching heart. These were welcome intermissions from the dramatic images that were on center stage in Tom's glass cubicle.

Brian, Teresa, and Kelli had arrived at the hospital a few hours before Steven. It was heart-warming to have everyone within hugging distance. Their willingness to come so far so quickly to share their concern deeply affected me. Love among family members was demonstrated in simple but profound ways. I was greatly touched by the caring each one showed the others. Together, all were comforting companions. It was a gift from God to have these beautiful people together.

Joe remembered Steven's musical talent, and brought his guitar to the hospital for Steven to play. At seventeen, Steven was already an accomplished musician, as well as a natural teacher for guitar students. He writes his own songs, and is gifted with an ear for either simple melodies or complex runs, and nimble fingers to make them all magically happen. With permission from the CCU nurse, Steven played softly next to Tom. He skillfully picked out tunes he had played many times for his enthusiastic father's ears.

As Steven played his dad's favorite Lynyrd Skynyrd tune, "Simple Man," Tom's tethered hands turned ever so slowly on the bed, and signaled a definite "two thumbs-up" gesture. My eyes widened at this surprising action, and I looked at Steven to see if he had noticed this movement. He had. Irrepressible smiles lit up our faces. This was the first indication of a mental connection between Tom and his surroundings. Tom had not yet awakened from his coma, and his face showed no expression, yet his hand signals showed that his brain was processing the moment. Joy and hope swelled in our spirits. It was still too early to know precisely how significant these small events might be, but my spirit silently sang praises to God. It hadn't been a fluke. Tom applauded his son with his thumbs-up acknowledgement several times as Steven played a repertoire familiar to them both.

That evening, Tom's color looked slightly better to me. I wondered if my natural longing to see him improve was overruling my perception of reality and was causing me to imagine a change. But when Dr. Sasso arrived, he confirmed my impression.

"He is still critically ill, but there has been some slight improvement."

Tom was in cardiogenic shock, with low oxygenation of tissues, acute renal failure, partial lung collapse, liver shock, and extremely low blood pressure—all critical conditions and serious failings of the body's systems. But the lactate and associated acidity was decreasing, and although there was still acute renal failure, kidney function had resumed minimally. This was a surprising reversal of the total renal failure recorded the day before. Another encouraging sign was that arterial pressure had increased to within normal range, indicating an improved circulatory picture. And although still sedated, Tom had opened his eyes momentarily in response to voice and moved his fingers and toes, showing better neurological response. Before Dr. Sasso left to see his other patients, he finished describing Tom's status with a phrase I will never forget, "He's not out of the woods yet; but there are fewer trees."

The word picture reminded me of a painting I had done years earlier of a path through a forest with sunbeams streaming through branches, lighting the way out. I couldn't help but think of my feet on that path and a familiar verse from the Bible:

"Thy Word is a lamp unto my feet and a light unto my path" (Psalms 119:105 ASV).

Chapter 5

Liberation Day

Mary Bee is a highly skilled and experienced nurse, and a close friend with a witty sense of humor. The "Bee" part of her name is an appropriate add-on that describes her energy level, and her self-proclaimed status as queen bee. We could count on a light-hearted atmosphere whenever we spent time together, and neither Mary nor Tom was ever at a loss for words during their lively repartees. Mary and her husband Nick's affection for Tom had generated the nickname they always used for him—"Tommy." Tom had never allowed anyone else to call him that, but it had quickly rolled off their lips, from early on, and it stuck. He would be "Tommy" to them.

Nick and Mary had come to the hospital immediately when they heard about Tom's sudden cardiac arrest. Nick, a retired Navy Seal, had stood next to Tom's bed, telling him he would pull through, calling him "Tommy." Tom was unresponsive but I knew it would be a comfort to him if he had any way to process the sounds that were in his room, and I thought gratefully how he would know exactly who was there by Nick's use of that name.

Mary Bee had come to see Tom every day since his admission to the hospital, and on this, the fourth day, her presence gave an added boost to the good news we heard from the CCU nurse. There was to be an important trial to see how well Tom might be able to breathe on his own without mechanical assistance. Oxygen levels in his blood had improved overnight and his pH had returned to normal range. It was determined that if Tom could cope with a gradual reduction of oxygen coming from the ventilator, then it would be advisable to remove the endotracheal tube. This would be an amazing advance and our hopes were high for its success.

Mary's arrival at this hour couldn't have been more timely. Brian was with me in Tom's room when the nurse informed us she had been given the go-ahead to remove the trach tube. Mary, with her experience in such things, wanted to stay with Tom during the process, and told us it would be good for him if we would stay also. She knew that Tom wouldn't understand where he was or why he needed to go through the ordeal he was about to experience. But he would recognize Brian's voice and hers, and would trust them to have his best interests at heart as they spoke to him to coach him through this difficult procedure. At the same time, Mary repeatedly assured us that Tom would not remember this experience later when he would be more alert.

The procedure began with a gradual reduction of oxygen being given through the tube, while monitoring Tom's ability to breathe with less help from the respirator. The oxygen was scaled back every 10 or 15 minutes, with continual observation. Tom was less sedated at this time in order for him to demonstrate he could breathe on his own. He was agitated with the tube—that was quite obvious. Mary assured us that agitation was normal and a good sign, attributable to increasing awareness and his ability to react.

His wrists were still tied to the bed rails with a little bit of length allowing some mobility, and he raised his hands as far as he could, but they weren't within reach of the breathing tube. If a patient were allowed to pull on the tube, it could cause great damage to the voice box as it bypassed it. Brian and Mary continued coaching Tom, reassuring him against his obvious agitation, and telling him what the procedure was. Brian took the lead and spoke to him, man-to-man, calmly, clearly, telling him this was important and encouraging him to continue.

I began to cave in with emotion. It was unbearable to me to see Tom in distress and not be able to relieve it. I left the room and moved where Tom wouldn't be able to see me through the glass door. Brian recognized my anguish and followed me out. He put his arms around me and I leaned into my tall, gentle son, lay my head on his chest, and stifled sobs. "I can't do this, Brian. I want to, but I can't do this."

"That's okay, Mom, you don't have to. I'll stay with Tom. You go into the waiting room. I'll come and get you when it's done."

I felt like I was abandoning Tom, even though I believed Mary when she said Tom wouldn't remember that I hadn't been there. How grateful I was for my son's compassion and strength. I thought how perfectly he exemplified his father at that moment—resolute, compassionate, and protective. Experiencing that unexpected flashback heightened the current drama, and my emotional reserve tank suddenly drained to "Empty."

I left the CCU and went to the Ladies restroom where all my stuffed composure broke through in exhausted sobs mingled with more emotions than I ever believed I could feel in one isolated moment. Relief at Tom's new level of improvement. Hope that his mental facilities would be adequate. Anguish over his struggle. Sorrow for his confusion about his circumstances and surroundings. Uncertainty about his recovery process—

what he would be able to do, think, say. Anxiety over how it would affect our relationship, our life together. These feelings would eventually sort themselves out, but it would be a while before I would have answers to the dozens of questions bombarding my emotions.

I went to the waiting room and joined Kathi, Joe, and Etta, and treasured friends who came to ask about Tom and to give me emotional support through their smiles, expressions of concern, and hugs. Larry and Barb Cobb stopped by on their way to the airport, not willing to let their important schedules keep them from assuring me of their love and prayers. David Wood came again to sit and chat, a solid rock. I marveled at his repeated visits. He had taken time away from his work each day to be with me for short, meaningful visits that washed my anxiety with waters of refreshed faith. His comfortable spirit of support was a true anchor in the storm. Marilyn Williams came by. Marilyn and Fred, long-time friends from McCall, had been of inestimable help and comfort to me for Pat's memorial service. Here she was again, a faithful friend at a cataclysmic time of my life.

Etta was there, dear Etta, Pat's mother. At age 88, she had booked a flight from Portland in order to be with me. Having heard the prognosis that Tom would not survive, she didn't want me to be alone and said she would stay for as long as I needed her. Etta is one of the most comfortable, loving people to be around that I know. My beautiful mother-in-law had blessed and welcomed Tom into the Donivan family with unconditional love, open arms, and open heart. In spite of Etta's home and ours being separated by 500 miles, she and Tom had developed a warm, fun-loving friendship through visits and phone calls. Tom loved to tease her, and she ate it up, laughing and teasing back.

All three of our church's pastors, Tim, Ed, and Volney, had come during the past four days. Mary and Jim Mitchell stopped by. They had opened their home to Steven and poured out their generous hospitality on him and his mother who had traveled with him. I could not have been in better company than with the family and friends who lavished their love upon us.

Together we waited. The minutes crept by slowly, but the cold hard edges of anxiety were softened by warm and loving words spoken in the waiting room. Finally, Brian came back from the CCU, smiling with relief and good news. "It's out," he announced. "He recognized me. He recognized Mary. He's doing great."

"Is he talking?" I asked breathlessly. I scrambled to my feet.

"Well, yes, a few words at a time, but his voice is very weak," Brian prepared me as I headed to the CCU. I couldn't wait to see Tom's face without the breathing paraphernalia and to see for myself that he really was "doing great." I hurried down the corridor, excitedly anticipating Tom's first verbal communication, no matter how brief it might be.

In the CCU, Mary Bee stood next to Tom's bed, holding his hand, and patting him on the shoulder. She was talking to Tom, smiling and gently teasing him in her customary way. Her sparkling blue eyes twinkled with joy. Her short blonde hair surrounded her smiling face like a halo.

I interrupted the one-way conversation with a kiss on Tom's liberated lips and cheeks, squeezed his hand, and with overflowing thankfulness said the only words I could think of, "I love you, Tom."

He responded with a murmured, "I love you." His voice was husky and labored. He was tired and closed his eyes. A few moments passed while Mary and I stood in silence and soaked in the celebration of the occasion. Then Tom broke the stillness with a quiet declaration, "Glory to God." Mary and I looked at one another, nodding in agreement. And a minute later, "I wanna go to glory." I understood his words, but struggled to process their implication—wondering if it was his clear and immediate wish to leave us again, right now. Wondering what he might have seen and heard during the time he was separated from us by unconsciousness. I had read credible stories of people with death experiences who told of such an experience in heaven that they were reluctant to come back to this life. With quiet conviction, Tom repeated, "I wanna go to glory." My exhilaration froze, arrested by sudden fear that he might not have the will to live after all his body had been through, or that he might be sensing the long road ahead I had been told to expect.

My fear was fueled by the realization that his body was still in a compromised status with obstacles in the path to recovery. His organs had shut down—kidneys, liver, respiration, brain, circulation, and it would be a challenge for these functions to return to full strength if indeed they would at all. I didn't have much time to contemplate the potential scenarios because Mary was filling me in on the details of Tom's recent liberation from the breathing tube.

"He recognized us, Marilee! As soon as the trach tube was out, the nurse pointed to me and asked Tommy, 'Do you know who this is?'" Mary's eyes filled with tears as she spoke. "And Tommy said, 'Tha's Mary, m' buddy.' Then pointing to Brian, she asked, 'Do you know who this is?' And without hesitation, Tommy said, 'Tha's Brian.'"

We looked at each other across the bed with moist eyes and beamed with relief and delight. We were basking in the goodness of God with joy that left us almost speechless.

As I stood, smiling at Tom and holding his hand between both of mine, he looked at each of us and formed words slowly and hoarsely, "Why'm I here? Wha' happen'?" His voice was weak and the words were slurred, but understandable. I paused, wondering how much Tom could take in about what had happened. How much should I tell him? Would it traumatize him and cause new problems?

His nurse smoothly took the lead and answered simply and directly, "You had cardiac arrest. Your heart stopped. You're in St. Luke's Hospital."

A minute or two later, Tom asked a second time, in a labored, husky voice, "Why'm I here? Wha' happen'?"

The nurse answered him again the same way, matter-of-factly, as though she had not heard the question a minute earlier. This same question/answer sequence repeated itself several more times, and my initial glee gave way to a sinking heart. How much memory/cognitive functioning did he actually have?

Mary saw my anxious eyes and reassured me softly from the opposite side of the bed. "It's the medication wearing off." Knowing I had enough to deal with for the time being, she wisely withheld describing other possible scenarios. She didn't tell me of her own concern that the current status might be the extent of his mental facility. It would be a while before we would have a clearer picture of his brain function.

For now, it was a time to rejoice in the blessing of his regained consciousness and recognition of faces. He had reached a crossing in the woods, and traversed it successfully.

He wasn't out of the woods yet, but again there were fewer trees.

Tom looked tired from the taxing effort of breathing on his own and the ordeal of the extubation.

"Do you want to go to sleep?" I asked. He nodded slightly and closed his eyes.

Mary and I left the room, and I anxiously quizzed her about what had taken place in the last hour while I sought refuge in the waiting room. I wanted to know what she, Brian, and Tom had experienced. She breathed a big sigh and said, "It's always tough to get through the removal of the trach tube, but Marilee, Brian was fabulous. I wanted us to be with Tommy during this tough procedure because he knows us and trusts us. I knew it would help him to see us and hear our voices. If I ever need a coach to get me through what Tommy just went through, I want Brian. He was just awesome. And I'm thrilled Tommy knows us. I've been holding my breath. This is a very good sign. After what he's been through, I didn't know if he would have any brain functioning. Marilee, this is a miracle."

I felt energized, ecstatic. It was a huge step forward. I shared the good news with friends back in the waiting room. Pastor Tim made a brief stop in Tom's room, prayed for him, thanked and praised the Lord, and spoke encouragingly to Tom, telling him God had brought him through. Etta stood at the foot of Tom's bed and greeted him. Tom looked surprised and enormously pleased to see her. "Etta... ," he drawled in his sluggish voice. "What're you doing here?" He raised his arms toward her and spoke in slow motion, "Come, gimme a hug." They embraced, and Etta's radiance clearly conveyed her thankfulness and delight at seeing him again.

Family and special friends were eager to take turns briefly seeing and speaking to Tom, and it was a little like musical chairs. With so little square footage in the room, people were coming and going in order to make room for the next one. It was a glorious celebration of subdued sounds for the sake of other patients, but with fireworks of joy in our hearts.

When Kathi squeezed into the room, we stood in a small half-circle around Tom's bed, marveling at seeing him with open eyes and breathing on his own. The nurse offered Tom ice chips to soothe his irritated throat. He softly rasped, "7-Up," but the nurse was firm.

"You need to start with ice, then you can have a little water. We want to see how you do before giving you 7-Up." Tom was insistent, but the nurse was just as resolute. She said, "I'll make you a deal. You start with this, and a little water, and then I'll bring you a 7-Up. Is that a deal?" The exchange reminded us of the current popular TV program, "Deal or No Deal", and we murmured something about that to one another, giggling. We felt relief and giddiness at Tom's emergence from the coma and his new freedom from the mechanical respirator. The nurse looked at me quizzically. "Deal or no deal?" she asked, puzzled at our inside joke.

I answered, "You know, that TV show, 'Deal or No Deal' with…who is that… ," I paused, trying to recall the name of the game host. While I searched my limited mind files of popular game show hosts, Tom filled in the blank.

"Howie Mandel," he croaked. Startled, four heads turned in unison and stared at the pillowed head as Tom entered into our frivolous conversation.

"What?" I asked, incredulously, thinking I could not have heard him correctly. He had provided the answer as if we were just munching cookies and chatting around a picnic table.

"Howie Mandel," he repeated, a little more forcefully. Astonished, we, his rapt audience, gaped at each other around the room and broke into joyful laughter. This was a very good sign indeed.

Chapter 6

Angels on Duty

I awoke early. It was Day Five. I could hardly wait to get to the hospital and see Tom again, anticipating improvement to continue, and thanking God with all my might for the astonishing changes. I followed the corridor between the Waiting Room and the CCU, a path now so familiar I knew exactly where my heels and toes would touch on the patterns of the carpeted floor. As required, I washed my hands at the entry sink, thinking my hands had never been so extraordinarily clean as they had been in the last five days through repeated soaping and scrubbing in my daily dozen trips to and from the CCU.

Tom was asleep, so I waited by his bedside, feeling enormously grateful and in awe of the changes I had witnessed since finding him lifeless on the floor of the living room in our home. I remembered the nurse's early Tuesday morning call that had propelled me to the hospital, and the moment I realized that it was possible, even probable, that I would not have the opportunity to greet Tom again as I was about to do. My heart was singing hallelujah choruses.

I took time to thank God again for the medical staff in St. Luke's CCU. Each person was extraordinary. I saw their dedication, professionalism, attentiveness, and compassion. They performed their tasks with sensitivity, and as I was praying aloud for Tom, I often included them in my prayers. I didn't ask for permission to pray for them, but simply added them to my prayers whether or not they were in the room, asking God to guide their observations and decisions, to help them in their pressing tasks, and to bless their personal lives, too.

As I stood beside Tom, I thanked God for Dr. Sasso, who was vigilant, persistent, intuitive, and knowledgeable. I reflected with gratitude on his willingness to spend as much time as I needed in order to help me understand the constantly changing situation. I had liked Dr. Sasso immediately at our first interaction. He has a rare ability to connect on a personal level even while delivering difficult information to patients and their stressed family members. Subsequent conversations had only increased my respect for his knowledge and dedication.

I prayed for David, the first RN who cared for Tom upon his emergency admission. When he had to leave his shift, I told him I wished he could be Tom's nurse for the duration. He said with sincerity, "I hope I get him again as my patient."

Shannon took over in the next shift and she was just as focused, professional, and attentive. We connected on a spiritual level, and exchanged words of faith, discovering we both knew Jesus Christ as our Savior. I thought how blessed Tom was to have really excellent, caring nurses.

Next, Jennifer came for her shift, and had such concern for her patient that she even dreamed about Tom, as she told me on the second morning of her assigned time in the CCU. I watched her care for Tom and marveled at the competence and compassion that he was receiving.

Then a fourth angel-nurse, Joanne, arrived for her shift. My appreciation for the high standards in the CCU grew with these continual and overlapping demonstrations of caring and competency. Joanne paused in her duties and bowed her head as I prayed for Tom and then for her. She thanked me afterward.

"Thank *you*," I said. "You have very difficult work, and are doing an amazing job."

It was warm consolation to watch these nurses and doctors. Each one was a comfort to me with their obvious expertise and personable demeanors. I felt that Tom was being given the best possible chance of a good outcome that I could ask for. God was clearly showing His love and provision through the medical professionals.

While I was contemplating these blessings, an industrious middle-aged lady with a round face and sweet smile entered the room with cleaning supplies. Her dress and the scarf around her head reminded me of Ukrainian women I had seen when I was in their country. I asked her if she needed me to leave the room so she could clean more easily. "No, it's alright. You stay here." Her answer had a Ukrainian accent. I looked at her hospital identification badge and saw "Nadia." I smiled and took a chance.

"Are you from Ukraine?" She beamed and nodded, and we exchanged a few more words. I told her about my visit to her country on a short-term mission trip and how I had sung songs with children and taught them about Jesus.

She nodded with understanding and said, "I pray for your husband." I was stunned. God sends his angels at surprising times in surprising attire! Deeply touched, I thanked her, took her hand, and said a prayer for her and for her family members who were still in Ukraine. As we finished our brief encounter, we both had tears in our eyes, recognizing a special moment in time had occurred. I marveled that some of the most meaningful times God gives us are when we are spontaneous and expressive in our tender-heartedness with strangers, and they with us.

As I reveled in God's provision and unexpected happenings, Tom opened his eyes. I greeted him with a kiss, a hug, and a heartfelt, "Oh, Tom, I LOVE you!"

In response, he murmured, "I love you, too," with a voice that had gained some strength from the night's rest, but was still slurred. He had, after all, been with limited oxygen in his brain for an extended amount of time, and I speculated he might have lingering after-effects similar to a patient recovering from a stroke. A quick picture of my early employment as a speech therapist in elementary schools flashed through my mind. I briefly considered the possibility that I would be working with Tom to help retrain his articulation. I can do that, I thought. I was grateful that I felt prepared for the task.

My galloping thoughts were interrupted by the nurse's entrance into the tiny room. She greeted Tom cheerfully and asked him how he was feeling. He indicated that he was uncomfortable with breathing. She showed no alarm, "You're having to work at breathing because your lungs were receiving oxygen passively through the ventilator for four days. It will feel like extra effort to breathe on your own until your lungs get used to it again. But it will improve," she added confidently. "You're doing well." She checked the oxygen monitor and was satisfied that his body was receiving sufficient oxygen in spite of his concerns. "You're at 100% oxygenation," she reassured him.

Dr. Sasso arrived outside Tom's cubicle with a small quiet crowd in white lab jackets. I was invited to attend the briefing of the medical team who stood, with their clipboards, looking at Tom through the glass wall. I stepped away from Tom in order to hear the report. It was a team of doctors and medical students, about eight in all. Dr. Sasso addressed each of the medical issues—Cardiovascular, Respiratory, Neurological, Renal, Endocrine, and Gastrointestinal. He noted updated labs, readings, and diagnostic tests. He specified the status and changes in each.

I listened intently, but much of his report was in specific medical terminology that was unfamiliar to me. Nevertheless, his finishing statement was clear. He paused, apparently reflecting on all the information he had just communicated. Slowly nodding his head, he wrapped up his assessment in two words:

"It's amazing."

Chapter 7

Party on the Seventh Floor

On Day Six, a Saturday morning, the cardiologist who had been assigned to Tom stopped by Tom's CCU room. He was wearing casual pants and a green polo shirt with the name of a team on it. Quick as ever to pick up on details, Tom asked him if he was on his way to a game. Yes, he was. He was the team's coach and his young son played on the team. Tom had coached his own son's team in football as well as Little League baseball, and began asking the doctor about his coaching experience. Part of Tom's journalism experience had been as a sports editor. He had conducted many interesting interviews with athletes and coaches at that time, and his interest in sports had not dwindled over the years.

Now he was in his standard mode of operation as he interviewed the cardiologist/coach. "How old is your son?" "Which do you like best—coaching on game day, or practice?" "How do you manage the parents who think their sons should be playing more?" And then, with a twinkle, "How many parents have you either shot or throttled?" Caught by surprise, the doctor looked startled, then laughed heartily, acknowledging the emotions of coaching competitive teams of children with fiercely competitive parents on the sidelines. I was both amused and amazed. The conversation was cohesive and interactive, each man exchanging relevant bits of information about their common experiences. Tom found out the doctor had been to Grand Junction, Colorado, liked both skiing and snow boarding, but preferred skiing. They took turns humorously describing their beginning snowboard antics. It was hard to believe Tom had been in a deep coma, dying, just three days earlier.

No doubt this spontaneous conversation affected the cardiologist as profoundly as it did me. Tom's remarkable cognitive functioning plus the day's blood tests showing levels of lactate, pH, enzymes, and electrolytes demonstrated enough improvement for him to be moved out of the CCU to the cardiac wing on the seventh floor of the hospital. He still sensed trouble with breathing, and fluid around and in the lungs was contributing to the problem. The possibility of pneumonia or an infection needed to be watched. In addition to respiratory therapy, cardiology recommended defibrillator implantation under the skin on his chest as a protective intervention in the case of a second episode of cardiac arrest. Statistically, fifty percent of patients who survive a sudden cardiac arrest will have a second one before they leave the hospital.

So with a greatly improved prognosis, Tom was moved by wheelchair to a room on the seventh floor for further monitoring, medication, and therapy to help him become strong enough for the implantation surgery. A second goal was for increased strength for heart bypass surgery. It had been found that he had at least three coronary arteries that needed bypass. Tom had lost 25 pounds in the six days since his cardiac arrest. He was very weak, unsteady on his feet, with pain and numbness in his right leg, presumably as a result of the femoral catheter that was placed at the time of his emergency admission. He would be doing some initial physical and respiratory therapy to further stabilize and strengthen his body before he could endure surgery.

Friends came by his room to rejoice over the move into this upper level room with a view. Their conversations were about answered prayers, then about topics Tom introduced through friendly inquiries. In the same inquisitive manner, Tom greeted and questioned nurses and staff that came to his room. Everyone was treated like a friend, teased a little, interviewed a little ("How's your day going?" "Hey, you got a haircut!" "What are you going to do this weekend?" "What do you think of…"), and always thanked for their work. Tom remembered each previous conversation and would pick up where he left off from the last time they had spoken together. The staff told me they looked forward to seeing him and having a cheerful conversation to brighten their day.

Dr. Sasso came upstairs to see Tom. They began to know each other a bit as Tom asked him about his background and family, and as they talked about the miracle of Tom's return to life. Dr. Sasso was clear in his explanation to Tom about it. Leaning against the wall near Tom's bed, he reviewed for Tom what he had just been through. He concluded with, "There is no medical or scientific reason for you to be alive."

The story was a mystery to Tom, but he confidently stated his own explanation. "It was the grace of God."

"Yes, it was the grace of God," the doctor agreed, nodding.

They talked a little bit about faith, and Tom told him how knowing Jesus Christ and following Him was of utmost importance to him. He said, "Most people want to know why things happen to them. I'm not asking God, 'Why me?' I'm asking God, 'Now that this has happened, what do you want me to do?'"

Tom's remarkable comeback was stunning to all who had cared for him. One of the CCU nurses came to the seventh floor during her break. She had been with Tom while he was comatose, so he didn't know her, but she was familiar to me. She was the pretty dark-haired Christian I had talked with. She brought with her a colleague, another young nurse. They came to the door of the room, all smiles, and paused politely at the entrance, waiting to be invited in. I immediately welcomed her and introduced her to Tom. She had not seen Tom since her shift while he was still comatose; and to see him now, eyes wide open, smiling, and conversing, was a joy she couldn't contain. She giggled with delight and introduced her colleague.

They were obviously excited and brought with them a party atmosphere. The medical staff of the CCU apparently had talked about Tom's unexpected recovery, and they wanted to see for themselves. It was a celebration, and Tom was the featured onstage star. They shared a brief but very animated conversation. Tom told them about Moses, a nickname he gave to the electrophysiologist with a booming voice and authoritative manner. "Yeah, when Moses comes into the room, you're pretty sure the waters are gonna part somewhere."

They laughed heartily, recognizing the characterization. "Oh, we've got to put that into the book!" The comment was memorialized in a book of light-hearted sayings the CCU staff reads, "when things get too heavy," they explained.

Physical therapy was an important component of Tom's time on the seventh floor. Tom's first challenge was to stand by the bed, then take just a few steps in the room while Jason, the physical therapist, held onto a belt around Tom's waist. For safety, Tom used a walker to steady himself for the first steps. True to Tom's style, he provided entertaining conversation, showing interest in Jason's course of studies, future plans, and current hobbies while they did some simple exercises and practiced walking.

Jason talked about his interest in art, especially in painting. At this piece of information, Tom's ears perked up. "Let me tell you about something you'd be interested in," he began, as his sales and marketing experience kicked in. Tom had been helping me market my beginning watercolor lessons and watercolor painting kits. He enthusiastically described the benefits and features of the products and very nearly made a sale during the course of his physical therapy. Jason asked me for my business card and website information, and said he would be checking it out.

Tom's room had a large east-facing window and the morning sun sent beams of light against the walls, a welcome greeting each cold February morning. At night, the view of Table Rock was ornamented by a lighted cross, a cherished Boise landmark that has been there for over half a century. Both mornings and nighttimes provided us beautiful reminders of the Source of the life that had been given back to Tom.

Tom spent two more weeks there and was able to have the defibrillator implanted by Moses, who proclaimed the procedure a flawless success. Then Tom was sent home to try to gain weight and strength for the upcoming heart surgery. Quintuple bypass surgery was completed four weeks later, beginning a new chapter in our lives—a new Normal—with a wondrous story to tell and lessons in faith for all seasons.

Chapter 8

What is Faith, Anyway?

Thoughts about the role of faith this morning ripple like a stream washing over and around rocks and curves in a riverbed. It has been over four years since Tom's resurrection. Seventeen years since Pat's home-going to heaven. Sometimes, significant insights, the life-altering kind, come after a period of incubation. I've pondered this for years, going around the various aspects of faith and God's sovereignty from different angles, puzzling over much of it. Prayerfully considering God's Word, examples in the Bible, and especially Jesus' words in the gospels concerning miracles and faith.

This morning, as Christmas celebrations and decorations were being packed up and put away for another year, I listened to the biblical account of the angel's visitation to Mary to announce the forthcoming miraculous world-changing event that she, a virgin, would become the bearer of the Son of God, the Savior of the world. As I considered the emotional faith challenges this presented not only to Mary, but also to Joseph, my mind leapt over the story's familiar details to find applications in my own life. A wonderful thing about faith is that it is full of new discoveries.

Faith makes possible, but faith does not control outcomes. God controls the outcome. We believe in Him, not in the miracle He performs. We believe in Him, not in the amount of faith we have. We are not to have faith in our faith. We are to have faith in God. He is to be our focus. As Pat frequently reminded me, what is important is not the miracle. What is important is God.

When a miracle occurs, praise and worship belongs to God, not to our faith. Messages like "you just need to have more faith" or "you didn't have enough faith" are not true to the Word of God. That message minimizes God's sovereign will and design. When Jesus said, *"Only believe"* and *"Because of your faith you are healed"* (Matt. 15:28, Mark 10:52), He was not affirming their faith for a miracle, or their self-effort of believing hard enough. He was affirming their faith in *Him*. That He was who He said He was, and that He was doing the Father's will.

"You believe in God. Believe also in Me." (John 14:1)
"Anyone who has seen me has seen the Father."(John 14:9)
"I and the Father are one." (John 10:30)

Jesus spoke clearly and directly about who He was. Some believed. Some did not. He performed miracles so that those who saw would believe who He was. Some people followed Him for the miraculous, perhaps somewhat like audiences are drawn to illusionists and performers, to be amazed, or perhaps to become a participant in a unique and miraculous event. Something to tell the neighbors about, to amaze and impress others, to talk about over coffee. And certainly, to receive relief from disease, hunger, disability, or demonic possession. This week, I have been reading in John, chapters 5-8, and pondering how people who witnessed these miracles didn't believe Jesus was who He said He was. What more proof could they have asked for? He even raised people from the dead. It was obvious to some. Denied by others. Some believed. Others would not.

These thoughts lapped at the edge of my mind, as deep questions of God's sovereignty swirled together with ponderings on the response of faith. Do we receive the message? Do we acknowledge the truth? Do we trust in God, and receive what He sends our way? Or do we contrive "a better plan" and obstinately pursue our own message, our own way? Do we brush aside the possibility that God will show us something greater than our own limited ideas, if we will just trust and wait for His answer?

This morning's broadcast message from Jack Hayford asked a tongue-in-cheek question regarding Mary's faith and preparation for the momentous announcement she was given by the angel. Hayford asked if we supposed Mary had taken the Scripture in Isaiah 7:14, saying to herself, "I believe this passage; I claim it for myself; I stand on Isaiah 7:14; and I *will* be the virgin from whom the Christ is born?"[1]

Of course, Hayford quickly assured his listeners that this is ludicrous. The very idea of Mary taking such an approach exaggerates a modern-day crack in some theologies. When placed in the context of another time and culture, we more quickly recognize it as a presumptuous and erroneous application of scripture. Something out of order in God's scheme of things. We can't take scripture out of context by claiming whatever we choose and expecting God to deliver it as if He owes us something. Yet, sometimes in our desperate need and desire for God's miraculous intervention, this deception slips in. It is a subtle error.

We cannot expect miracles to be delivered as if from an ATM machine simply because we plug in faith and claim scriptures as our own. God's Word is true, yes. Believing its Truth, we stand firmly on the principles of His Word. But God's Word is not a book of formulas, nor a book of positive thinking, fantasy, or self-hypnosis. Not a one-size-fits-all-for-every-situation book. We do not flippantly claim scriptures foolishly. Instead we prayerfully read the Scriptures, asking God to give us His point of view, His will. Jesus sets the divine example:

"And He was saying, Abba! Father! All things are possible for You; remove this cup from Me; yet not what I will, but what You will," he cried (Mark 14:36). We believe God, have faith in His goodness and wisdom, and trust Him, always remembering His sovereign love and wisdom may have designed and ordained a different path for us than the one we envision.

It is not the power of our faith that brings miracles to come to pass. It is the power of God, and His sovereign plan. This is certainly a good thing, because no matter how hard we try, we cannot manufacture a greater measure of faith as if it's a commodity. "If I just give it a little more effort, maybe I can believe harder," we wish. We can wear ourselves out trying to increase our faith. Faith is a gift from God. *"No man can come to Me, except the Father draws Him."*(John 6:44)   Faith is given to us by measure through the Holy Spirit. For *"the fruit of the Spirit is love, joy, peace, faith..."* (Gal. 5:22). Whatever God gives us is enough. He does not expect us to act outside of His provision. However much faith we have is enough for what He calls us to do. But we must use what He gives us, for *"without faith it is impossible to please God. Whoever comes to God must believe that He is, and that He is a Rewarder of those who diligently seek Him"* (Heb. 11:6). The Bible says when we come to God, all we are asked to do is two things:

1. Believe that He is. He exists. He lives, and breathes, and loves, and acts. Believe God, rely on Him; do not rely on how much *faith* we have; rely on GOD.

2. Believe that He is a Rewarder as we truly seek Him. His reward, whatever is best, is sovereignly chosen and given to us according to the need He sees. And He sees so much more than we do.

God IS, and He rewards us as we seek Him, lean on Him, and trust Him! We need not be afraid or reluctant to ask for big things. We are encouraged in Hebrews 4:16, *"Let us therefore come boldly before the throne of grace, that we may obtain mercy, and find grace to help in time of need."* God understands our weakness, and provides us grace. We are urged to come boldly to Him for whatever our need is, even if it is to say, *"Please help my unbelief!"* (Mark 9:24).

Yes, God does miracles today. Sometimes they are clearly visible to others, even to unbelievers. Some may say, "It is a miracle that..." They may see that something is beyond normal activity and natural forces. But they shrug it off, knowing it is a mystery, and don't ponder or consider the source of the miracle.

"How did such a thing happen? Did some personal force cause it, or was it just 'luck'? Hm, I'll figure it out later," seems to be the attitude. Meanwhile, life's demanding issues steal attention from the underlying question, "How did this happen?" and more significantly, "Who made this happen?"

The role of faith, I believe, is to learn who Jesus is, and submit our lives, our ways, our outcomes, to His plan for us. When we do this, regardless of the various events, surprises, or disappointments along our path, God smiles on us and says, *"Well done, good and faithful servant"*(Matthew 25:21). My role is to learn the "Who" part of God. And let Him declare and bring about the "what's" and "how's" of my life.

This is by no means a passive approach to my relationship with God. By reading His Word, taking time to study its meaning, and praying for understanding, I learn, day by day, year by year, how gracious, kind, loving, wise, and good He is. Again and again, He reveals His character, power, and personal love for us in hundreds of ways and circumstances. Each time we pray and see His answers, our faith is strengthened to rely on Him for the next need. And to thank Him for His faithful provision and presence with us, no matter what we face.

This morning during our coffee date, Tom and I talked about his "cocoon" experience. "In a cocoon" is the descriptive phrase he gives to the time he was in a coma. It is remarkable, because when I had called my praying friend, Molly, to tell her of Tom's sudden cardiac arrest and that he was in a deep coma with a high risk of mortality, Molly made a startling statement. After she had listened without interruption, she said, "Marilee, Tom is going to be okay. God has him in a cocoon. He's in a cocoon, and he's going to come out like a butterfly."

A cocoon is dark, quiet, isolated, and amazingly strong. It protects its precious contents against storms and threats from the outside world. It is a place of insulation, warmth, and transformation. How Tom describes his "cocoon" is, "It was warm and full of life, with a sense of God's presence there. I didn't see anything, or hear anything. I just had the sense of being in a quiet environment of life and warmth."

Talking about the cocoon reminded us of a profound lesson in prayer, a mysterious one that we dare not try to unravel with too much analysis. It was an unusual and holy revelation, describable as a gem in God's unsearchable riches. It became apparent shortly after Tom had emerged from his "cocoon," and was being cared for on the cardiac floor of the hospital. I was spending time with him there when he received a phone call from a good friend. In their conversation, I heard Tom refer to his sense of having been in a cocoon. Because he was on the phone, I had no opportunity to tell him about Molly's comment, so I just listened in amazement and waited eagerly for the conversation to finish. As Tom further described his experience, he repeated the phrase, this time adding a new detail. "I felt like I was in a warm cocoon, and it was full of life, life, life."

I was stunned. My eyes widened, and my heart thumped with joy when I heard him describe a cocoon and oddly repeat "life, life, life" in that context. It was precisely how I had prayed for Tom the first night he was in the hospital after I had returned home and lay emotionally exhausted in bed, trying to grasp the reality of what I had experienced in the preceding hours. As I had prayed aloud in the darkness, faith arose, and my voice strengthened with conviction as I spoke, "Lord, You are Lord of life. My life is yours, and Tom's life is yours. All things are subject to You and Your Name, and I praise and thank You that You are in this with me. You have given us authority in Jesus' Name. And in Jesus' Name, I speak Life,

LIFE, LIFE into Tom's body right now! In the Name of JESUS!" I had been startled by the imperative tone of my voice, and the boldness to speak such a thing, but I felt no sense of impropriety. Then, feeling that everything was released into the loving hands of God, I went to sleep.

These are mysterious workings of the Spirit. He gives us His words to pray and impressions of supernatural workings we cannot know outside of His tender revelation and our bold, willing response. *"For it is God who works in you both to will and to do His good pleasure"* (Philippians 2:13). He teaches us and leads us into new faith territory as we walk with Him. *"Jesus is the author and perfecter (completer) of faith"* (Hebrews 12:2). This is not hocus-pocus, crystal ball stuff. This is authentic communication from the Spirit of God according to His timing and will for us. It is not a usual event. If it were, we would take it for granted and treat it far too lightly. God reserves these astonishing moments for specific and needful times. And it takes our breath away.

As we sipped our coffee, I told Tom how I remembered his "cocoon time" from my external view of his coma. Recalling it brought tears to my eyes. I had been fully aware that Tom was in limbo, beyond my ability to communicate with him. But as I stood beside his paralyzed body, I was also fully, wonderfully aware that Tom was in a time and place where God had exclusive access to him. No distractions, no busyness. It was precious communion time with Him. I was grieving over the cardiac arrest and the fragility of Tom's condition being kept alive only by mechanical means and a mere silken thread strung between heaven and earth. Yet I was keenly aware that God was ever present, and very much involved in all that was happening, not only in the Critical Care Unit, but deep within Tom's inner spirit.

I thought of God's faithfulness to His children, how He has *"plans for good, and not for evil, plans to give us a hope and a future"* (Jeremiah 29:11). I contemplated conversations and experiences Tom and I had shared in the four years we had known and loved each other. I pondered the sadness and anger Tom's young heart had experienced when his earthly father deserted his family, then caused more pain when he had made a few unwelcome appearances during Tom's boyhood. I prayed Tom would feel the affectionate, affirming warmth of his Heavenly Father in a very real way, something he had not had from his earthly father. I longed for a holy, precious time for Tom and his Abba Father in that quiet, mysterious place that only God could touch. I had felt a strong sense that this was to be the focus of my prayers.

Friends and family had joined me in praying for Tom's return to health and life—all of us knowing we were asking God for a miracle. And why not? Jesus, the miracle worker, urges us to come boldly before the throne of God to ask and find help in time of need (Hebrews 4:16). God desires to show His power and glory. Which miracle would be the greater? God knew. Perhaps life restored. Perhaps Fatherly Love received in a new dimension. Either would be a magnificent event, bringing God glory and honor.

My daughter, Kathi, spent hours with me in the CCU waiting room, chatting with friends who stopped by, and occasionally checking in on Tom, hoping to see some positive change. The morning of the second day, she arrived with a small package. Inside the wrapping was a plaque with a Bible verse she and I had clung to during her father's illness. Hebrews 11:1 was beautifully written in decorative script. *"Faith is the substance of things hoped for, the evidence of things unseen."* My heart was deeply touched, for we two were once again together believing God for a miracle, with the memory of a miracle we had prayed for years earlier for her father but did not see come to pass.

With her purchase of the plaque, Kathi had taken a bold step of faith, willing to cast everything on Jesus, as before. She embraced His Word, as before, believing God to be very present and willing to hear our prayers and see our faith directed toward His wisdom and goodness in the face of dire, even impossible, circumstances. She told me she had to overcome a sense of fear when she purchased it, and had resolved she would not be deterred by the "what if" of the looming threat of Tom's death. She deliberately pushed aside temptations of fear and negative thoughts which argued against leaning on God's Word again for another experience of fiercely held faith. Her courage and faith thrilled me. I was stunned by her resolute stance, and by her trust that I would be as inspired as she was by the scripture. I was blessed by her vulnerability and submission to the Spirit of Christ as He directed her to "Believe still! Believe again!"

We will not be desolate when we lean on our faithful God and wonderful Savior, trusting His answers, even though they may not be the answers we expect. Desolation comes when we rely on our own interpretation of what ought to be, and see our self-made plans fall apart. We are mystified and in despair only when we insist we know the best plan, and then it fails to materialize.

The marvelous goodness of God, however, is our unsinkable life preserver. Knowing the life preserver is designed for a specific purpose and is fail-proof, we can cling to it while treading the deep waters of disappointment and disillusionment. We have to reach for it and hold on. It will hold us up until the ultimate rescue is completed with relief and restoration. Only God can accomplish this for us. He reaches down, takes us in His lap, and with His strong arms around us, tells us He has it in His control and all will be well. We only need to wait a little while. And hold on.

"Let perseverance finish its work so that you may be mature and complete, not lacking anything" (James1:4).

FLASHBACK

Sometimes following a traumatic event, details that preceded the catastrophe come to mind with new meaning. A few days before Tom's sudden death, he and I had been in a local coffee house with one of the pastors of our church. Tom was earnestly speaking of his desire to use his spiritual gifts to serve God, and to help other believers do the same. The conversation was striking to me, hearing Tom very concisely and fervently express this with an earnestness that was unusually strong. His face glowed with enthusiasm and inner conviction as he spoke. It so impressed me, that I told him afterward, "Tom, God is doing something in you. I don't know what it is, but I saw something different about you as you spoke to Ed. God has something going on in you. I'm excited to see what it is going to be, how it is going to play out." I paused, waiting to see his reaction.

He nodded. "Yes, I know. I feel God is working something out, too. But I honestly don't know what it is. We'll just have to wait and see." Because the exchange took place just prior to his cardiac arrest, short term memory loss (a common result of oxygen deprivation to the brain) doesn't allow Tom to remember it. But I vividly remember both the conversation and my impression as he spoke. I have wondered about it many times since, and have prayed about its significance, seeking some understanding. I believe I saw a visible sign of God's Spirit at work in Tom preparing him for something that would demand more from him than ever before.

"Behold, I will do a new thing; now it shall spring forth; shall ye hot know it? I will even make a way in the wilderness, and rivers in the desert" (Isaiah 43:19 KJV).

Although I still have questions, bits of understanding come in glimpses, not complete pictures. Cocoon glimpses. Some things are not meant to be understood all at once. I might miss the full meaning if I were given everything all at once. Instead, I believe God gives us a limited number of snapshots bit by bit along the way so we can savor each one's details, and spend time contemplating and talking to God about it. God loves our company and welcomes our questions and conversations. *"Draw near to God and He will draw near to you"* (James 4:8). We are still in process. Later, perhaps in heaven or perhaps before, we will be shown the expanded panorama of His marvelous work. And it will wow us.

Chapter 9

Paper Tigers

I used to tremble at the thought of demonic forces in the world, especially when I was told they are not limited to certain geographic locations. It bothered me to think that I was a target of Satan because of my life in Christ. It seemed spooky and scary to me, and I felt like I needed to be ready to duck and dodge the attacks somehow, but I didn't know how. It doesn't scare me any longer. We don't have to duck or dodge. That is a picture of being on the defensive, but it's the wrong picture. The right picture of a Christian's defensive posture is to be alert and to stand firm, holding up the shield of faith—"*taking up the shield of faith with which you will be able to extinguish all the flaming arrows of the evil* one"(Ephesians 6:16). The Bible empowers us by exposing our enemy, revealing his tactics, and reminding us he was once and for all defeated through the cross of Christ. For Christians, the enemy is only a paper tiger.

> "And having disarmed the powers and authorities, He made a public spectacle of them, triumphing over them by the cross" (Colossians 2:15). (NIV)

The wording here is exultant. In this context, "the powers and authorities" are references to the organized spirit world of darkness. These enemies were disarmed at the cross. To disarm is to strip away weapons and render powerless—and what is an army without weapons?

In addition to being disarmed, the enemies, Satan's demons, were publicly exposed as they suffered their undoing. The cross was a public event viewed by men and angels. Satan, in his evil pride and inability to understand the great love of God, erroneously thought he had won when Jesus died. Instead, it was Satan's own crushing defeat and heaven's triumph over his wicked plans.

For believers in Christ, the devil's works to rob, kill, and destroy have been rendered null and void by the work of our Lord. Our glorious Savior took the full brunt of every sin on

His own body. Every particle of our lives that was formerly controlled by Satan's dominion over us is now under the blood and dominion of Christ. *"The law of the spirit and life in Christ Jesus has made me free from the law of sin and death"* (Romans 8:2). Christ gave The Final Answer. *"For this reason the Son of God was manifested, that he might destroy the works of the devil"* (I John 3:8).

The devil cannot undo the restoration that Christ provides for every person who will receive God's forgiveness through the cross. Jesus' willingness to be our substitute and suffer the punishment we deserve is the amazing provision of the Righteous Judge so that we, who are willing to accept His gift, can go free. The penalty was paid. *"It is finished"* (John 19:30).

I revel in the final phrase of Colossians 2:14, *"triumphing over them by the cross."* I like the word "triumph." It's the pinnacle of celebration when the underdog comes from behind at the last minute and scores the final point, winning a fiercely contested tournament. And the triumph Paul refers to is far greater than a world tournament win; for it is a contest between good and evil, a contest for men's souls, and the triumphant celebration will resound in heaven throughout eternity.

The apostle Paul tells us how to use the weapons Christ has given us to enforce His victory over the enemy. Many times I have used the *"weapons of our warfare which are mighty through God to the pulling down of strongholds, casting down imaginations and every high thing that exalts itself against the knowledge of God..."* (2 Corinthians 10:4-5). We have ample provision against the schemes of the devil. Learning this has remodeled and strengthened my faith.

As believers in Christ, when we have determined in our hearts and minds that we will follow Jesus and that we want to please God, we will experience opposition. The Bible tells us the forces exerted against our faith are the world, the flesh, and the devil. In our western world where we are primarily analytical and scientific in our orientation, we are not as quick as people in eastern countries to recognize spiritual forces that are assembled against us.

Missionaries in other countries commonly see assaults of evil spirits against people and cultures. The Jesus Film Ministry teams, as they travel to share the gospel around the world, often encounter witch doctors and demon-controlled tribal leaders. The Film teams, trained in the Scriptures, have proven the power and authority of the name of Jesus as they meet fierce opposition. There is no doubt God has given His children protection and equipped us against attacks from our enemy, the devil.

The devil takes advantage of us, especially when we are tired, stressed, sick, or discouraged. When Tom was in the hospital, I experienced two weird manifestations of this. In our backyard, we have a beautiful water feature that is a rock formation with a waterfall in the center. Water cascades over the tiered levels and splashes into our man-made pond which holds about 800 gallons of water. A pump steadily re-circulates the water to create a picturesque retreat with a soothing sound. Normally everything runs like clockwork.

On the fourth morning of Tom's hospitalization, I walked into the kitchen to get a cup of coffee for my trip to the hospital. Instinctively, I looked out the kitchen window which has a wide view of the water feature. I always feel blessed by this first look at the outside world. The early morning light and shadows play off the evergreens and multicolored boulders in contrasting colors and textures. It reminds me that God is all about creating beauty—a thought that never ceases to refresh my spirit.

On this particular morning, the water spilled over the boulders, splashing in dance-like movements as it bounced from rock to rock; but I couldn't see the surface of the water in the pond. I slid open the glass door to the patio and went out to peer over the edge of the low rock wall surrounding the pool of water. There was no pool of water. The pump was drawing water from under the lowest layer of rocks at the very bottom of the pond. No longer a pond, overnight, it had become just a basin filled with rocks.

I was shocked. This was a first. I looked around for indications of where 800 gallons of water had gone, and there were no soggy spots that would suggest a leak around the pond wall, the liner, or the landscaping that surrounds the pond. When I realized that the pump was still pumping water, I thanked God it had not burned out; there was still just enough water to keep it going without sustaining damage. I thought, I don't have time to deal with this now. I'll just turn off the pump, and figure this out later. I needed to get to the hospital.

When I came home, I inspected the site again, still puzzling over what had happened to allow the pond to go nearly dry. I could not detect anything out of the ordinary. Thanking God again for preserving the life of the pump, I considered the source of this odd emptying. Obviously the pump was working well, so that wasn't the problem. I decided I would leave the pump turned off, fill the pond with water again, and watch to see what would happen. I unreeled the garden hose and began filling the pond, studying the results as I did so, watching for any sign of leaking. Since no problem developed, I decided to wait until morning to see if the water level would change overnight as it had the night before. I left the pump turned off and went to bed.

In the morning the water level was the same. I began to get an inkling of the source of the problem. It wasn't the pump. It wasn't the liner. It wasn't the basin. It wasn't anything physically discernable. There was no reason for the pond to have drained dry. It was simply spiritual harassment from the enemy of faith. It was meant to be a distraction, something to disrupt peace and faith in our miracle-working God who was *"showing Himself strong on behalf of those whose heart is loyal to Him"* (2 Chronicles 16:9), in Room 101 of the CCU.

I stood outside next to the water feature and said, "Father, I praise You that You always win. I stand in the strong name of Jesus against all enemy spirits that try to interfere with what You are doing in my life and in Tom's. I refuse to be distracted or discouraged by this event. In Jesus' strong and mighty Name I declare victory in every part of my life." Then I addressed the enemy. "You, deceitful spirits, have no place here. My life is in Jesus Christ, and you have no power over me or my property. I will not be upset. I do not accept your interference. So get out of here in Jesus' name!" With that settled, I knew I could turn the pump back on and run it as usual. It has been running without a problem ever since.

Paul tells us how to make use of God's provisions for spiritual warfare. He emphasizes that once we have the armor of God and actually put it on (by faith and conscious awareness that it is our provision), we will be able to stand against the onslaughts of the enemy. *"Put on the whole armor of God that you may be able to stand against the wiles of the devil"* (Ephesians 6:11).

A second occurrence of spiritual harassment came a few days later. This time it involved the garage door. Tom was still in the hospital. He had improved to the point that he had been moved out of the CCU into the cardiac wing on the hospital's seventh floor, but was still in jeopardy with respiratory challenges, compromised organs, and the possibility of another heart incident. As usual, I planned my day around his schedule, and left the house early with a cup of coffee and a piece of toast in hand. I backed the car out of the garage and closed the garage door, using the remote control. I watched the door engage and close completely, taking extra care to ensure things were buttoned up and safe for Etta. She had decided to take a break from the hospital and stay at the house to rest and work on some embroidery.

As I drove to the hospital, I thanked God for her love and willingness to be with me in the mornings and evenings, knowing she had plenty of things in her own home which she always enjoyed, and many friends and the rest of the family to spend time with in Oregon. Her selfless and comfortable companionship was a refreshing oasis in the midst of deep concern about Tom's ever-changing physical needs.

When I returned from the hospital, Etta told me that Jim, our neighbor across the street, had come over to ask if she knew the garage door was up. Jim knows we don't leave our garage door open unless we are working in the yard, and he could see that the car was gone, so he figured there might be a problem. Etta guessed that I had forgotten to close the door in my haste to see Tom. She said she had told Jim, "Thank you so much for coming over. But I don't know how to get the door to go down." Jim had taken her into our garage and had shown her the control button on the wall. The door was lowered at the press of the button, and Jim went back across the street. Etta finished her story, commenting on how glad she was that we have such thoughtful and attentive neighbors.

I agreed. Then I asked her, "Did you use the button on the wall to open the door a second time? It was open when I drove up."

She looked surprised. "No, I didn't touch it after Jim left."

"Are you sure?" I wanted her to remember some reason she had opened the door again.

She was adamant. "No, I didn't need to open the door for anything."

"Well, that's really strange. And I know the door was closed before I drove away this morning. I watched it come down." We left the mystery unsolved at that point, because there were more important things to talk about.

I went back into the garage a little later to check on things, and the door was up again. I sighed with exasperation and closed it. Then I remembered the exercise I had gone through with the pond just days before. I sensed this door problem was another act of demonic harassment.

I stood in the garage and spoke to the unseen force I believed was creating this annoyance. "I reject your harassment, spirits of darkness. I belong to the Lord, the One who made heaven and earth and everything in it. All things and all beings are subject to His name, and in the name of Jesus Christ, I forbid you to continue this harassment. This garage door will stay down. There is nothing wrong with it. Leave now, and don't come back." There were no further incidents with the door.

In times past, I have felt a little silly speaking to what appears to be empty air. But the Bible tells us there are spirits around us all the time, some for good and some for evil. Spiritual battles are fought in the spiritual realm. Just because we can't see it doesn't negate its reality. I believe the Bible reveals this truth to us so that we can walk in wisdom and in the power of the name of Jesus Christ no matter what is confronting us. God wants us to be informed in our faith, and armed against forces that come against us, whether they are people, circumstances, out-of-control emotions, or spirit beings.

There have been times that I spoke to something, calling on the name of Jesus, mistaking it for a spiritual battle when it wasn't. But that doesn't bother me. If I have not discerned correctly, nothing is lost. I laugh at a recent example. It also involved the pond. I was annoyed at the outlet not working when I plugged in the pump's electrical cord after draining and cleaning the pond. I had been trouble-shooting and testing every way that I could figure. Nothing made the GFI outlet work. I then spoke boldly to the situation in the name of Jesus, and found out soon after that the mistake was my oversight. I didn't have the controlling switch on! So, spiritual discernment is sometimes flawed by our limited understanding not only in spiritual realms, but also in physical ones. I still chuckle at that experience.

I am not deterred from fighting against unseen forces when it appears to be called for, even at the risk of being wrong. Satan would love to keep us intimidated and impotent by our fear of being potentially embarrassed. I would rather speak it and be wrong, than be wrong and not speak it when it was really needed. I've been told that practice in this arena increases our discernment. I'm finding that to be true.

Another scenario presented itself about seven months after Tom's quintuple bypass heart surgery following his recovery from the sudden cardiac arrest. He had gained sufficient strength to feel ready to take on a ministry he was previously involved in, a ministry to inmates in a medium security prison. It was a weekend event, and Tom took our car to drive to the location. We had only one car at the time, but I didn't mind being home without a vehicle. I felt it would be a perfect time to be "grounded" because I planned on concentrating in prayer for the prison ministry, and didn't want to be distracted by leaving the house for any reason.

What I didn't plan on was the smoke alarm fiasco. The alarms began to sound off on Saturday, the day I knew was a pivotal time for the inmates who were hearing about the love of God and being given an opportunity to receive Jesus Christ into their lives. At the sound of the first smoke alarm I waited a few seconds to see if it was something that would go away shortly. It didn't, so I got out of my chair to investigate. As I navigated through the house, just when I thought I had identified the specific alarm that was activating, the sound would shift to another room. This occurred repeatedly as I went from room to room. It was ear-piercingly shrill. And it was quirky. I couldn't nail the spot because it kept moving.

I thought, Oh, great. No car. I can't even leave the house to get away from this racket! It was November, too cold to sit outside. I was aggravated. Then I put two and two together. Aha. Here I am, praying earnestly, while Tom is telling hurting men about Jesus. This is no coincidence that this interruption is happening right now. I think I get it. I went into the garage and turned off the circuit breaker marked "Smoke Alarms." I thought, That'll fix it. But the cacophony continued. Altogether, the elements seemed to add up to demonic activity, and I planted my feet, raised my fist, and almost shouted over the din, "I'm onto you, you spirits of hell. You will not prevent me from praying. You will not interfere with God's plan for this day. You may not continue this harassment. In the name of Jesus, I command you to shut off this noise, and leave this place right now. Go! In the name of Jesus!" The noise stopped, except for one last short beep, like a petulant child kicking the dirt. Peace was restored and I praised God for His absolute supremacy.

Times when mechanical things have been instruments to distract, annoy, and frustrate me have taught me one very important truth. The demons have no power over *me,* because I am indwelt by the Holy Spirit, the Spirit of Christ. They can't hurt me, unless I give them a foothold through compromise or outright disobedience to God. The best they can do is mess with things *around* me. That is an overriding, powerful comfort. Evil spirits that aligned with Satan when Satan rebelled against God are no match for Almighty God who created them, or for those of us who bear the name of Jesus Christ and live under His authority in humility and submission to Him. When Jesus' commissioned seventy disciples to go ahead of him into cities, he sent them with authority to heal the sick. It is evident that they faced demonic forces in some of their experiences, for when they returned and reported to Jesus, they were elated. *"Even the demons are subject to us in Your name!"* Understanding their amazement and joy, Jesus confirmed their experiences, saying,

> *"I saw Satan falling like a lightning flash from heaven. Behold! I have given you authority and power to trample upon serpents and scorpions, and [physical and mental strength and ability] over all the power that the enemy [possesses]; and nothing shall in any way harm you"* (Luke 10:19 AMP).

Serpents and scorpions are used symbolically in the Bible to represent the enemy—Satan, and spirits of darkness. Jesus acknowledged his disciples' excitement that the spirits had to obey them, but went on to remind them that they had an even greater reason to rejoice because their names were written in heaven. *"Nevertheless, do not rejoice at this, that the spirits are subject to you, but rejoice that your names are recorded in heaven"* (Luke 10:20). Without their solid connection with power from heaven, there would be no power over demonic spirits.

At the core of this important statement is remembering we speak not in our own authority, but in the authority of the name of Jesus. Jesus instructed His disciples to remember that power for all He gave them to do came from Him.

*"I am the vine, you are the branches; he who abides in Me and I in him, he bears much fruit, **for apart from Me** you can do **nothing**"* (John 15:5).

Jesus now has conferred His authority upon us so that we can live in this world undaunted by demonic interference. Christ alone has power over these forces. I have no authority in myself. My authority or power is from Jesus, so I speak in His name.

A time is coming when spirits as well as men will be judged by the righteous judge, Jesus. Satan knows his time is short, and he is ferociously stepping up his game.

"Woe for the earth and for the sea: because the devil is gone down unto you, having great wrath, knowing that he hath but a short time" (Rev.12:12).

We, his targets, need to step up our game, too, and be informed and confident in the Word of God about who we are, what our defensive and offensive weapons are, and how to use them. As we look around, and watch world news, we have horrifying exhibits of the evil that is infiltrating every aspect of human and political life. The enemy of God can do no damage to the Most High God, Creator of the universe, so Satan and his demons attempt to neutralize the work of God and His beloved children by keeping us ignorant of his devices and deceiving us into feeling helpless in the face of them. He is the father of lies, Jesus tells us. We read it in the gospel of John. Speaking to the unbelieving Jews, Jesus emphatically declares,

> *"You are of your father the devil, and you want to do the desires of your father. He was a murderer from the beginning, and does not stand in the truth because there is no truth in him. Whenever he speaks a lie, he speaks from his own nature, for **he is a liar and the father of lies**"* (John 8:44).

We need to be doers of the Word in this unfamiliar territory and not hearers only. And God has provided us everything we need for success. It is our divine equipment to have the Word of God firmly established in our hearts and God's spiritual armor protecting us, as the apostle Paul instructs us:

> *10 "Finally, be strong in the Lord and in the strength of His might.*
> *11 Put on the full armor of God, so that you will be able to stand firm against the schemes of the devil.*

12 For our struggle is not against flesh and blood, but against the rulers, against the powers, against the world forces of this darkness, against the spiritual forces of wickedness in the heavenly places.

13 Therefore, take up the full armor of God, so that you will be able to resist in the evil day, and having done everything, to stand firm.

14 Stand firm therefore, having girded your loins with truth, and having put on the breastplate of righteousness,

15 And having shod your feet with the preparation of the gospel of peace;

16 In addition to all, taking up the shield of faith with which you will be able to extinguish all the flaming arrows of the evil one.

17 And take the helmet of salvation, and the sword of the Spirit, which is the word of God.

18 With all prayer and petition pray at all times in the Spirit, and with this in view, be on the alert with all perseverance and petition for all the saints..." (Ephesians 6:10-18).

It is not enough to have this passage memorized and in our intellectual storage unit. We need, as Paul said, to put on the full armor of God, and having done all, to stand. Stand firm. The exhortation to stand firm comes repeatedly in his instructions. It is a valuable reminder that our strength is in Christ's provision, and it is His armor that we wear, not our penetrable self-made protection. Because of Christ alone we are safe while we stand firm against the enemy.

This is how we are to be strong in the Lord and in the power of His might. When we are acting in faith, trusting God's Word, and taking action with a pure heart, we are not alone. We are attached to the Vine, and His life and strength flows through us to accomplish His will. He is always with us. No battle needs to be fought on our own.

> *"All authority is given unto me in heaven and in earth,"* said Jesus, just before He ascended into heaven. *"Go ye, therefore, and teach all nations...to observe all things whatsoever I have commanded you; and lo, I am with you always, even unto the end of the age. Amen"* (Matthew 28:19-20 ASV).

Chapter 10

Remembering and Forgetting

Trinkets and treasures. Trinkets are generally thought of as trivial or unimportant. When we lose a trinket, we may not realize it right away. When we become aware of its disappearance, it is only a "ho hum" problem. Trinkets can be replaced easily and inexpensively by another trinket.

It is a very different experience with a treasure. A treasure may have been received as a gift from someone precious to us, and the giver is the reason the item is a treasure. Sometimes a treasure was fiercely fought for with perseverance, courage, and honor. How it was won is part of its precious nature.

Because we highly value it, we pay attention to it. We think about how to keep it safe. If we lose it, we grieve its loss.

Faith is a treasure, not a trinket. We value it highly because of the Giver and the price that was paid in order to transfer it to us. To keep it safe, we need to give it our attention and protection. There are times in every life when faith is pushed to the limits and we fear its loss over the edge of a calamitous cliff. When we are battling for faith, there are two things we can do to wrestle it back to safety. We can remember and we can forget.

Remembering

When our faith is in jeopardy, it's a good time to remember our miracles. Many of us have had a "wow" moment when we knew something happened because God intervened in some way to protect us or provide for us, to heal, or to show us something we needed to see. It was unusual. It was timely. It was better than we expected. It was beyond our control. What a marvel it was! What joy we had in telling others! But do we remember it every day? Perhaps not.

Now, almost five years after the event, I think many of our friends and family may have forgotten how miraculous it was when Tom came back to consciousness with good mental functioning and then slowly regained physical vitality and mobility. It had taken some time for his internal organs to "remember" what they were designed for. The first part of the multi-organ system failure was that his digestion system had completely quit working, and even while he had tried to gain weight, he had lost 40 pounds in the month following the cardiac arrest. The doctor had told him to eat "anything and everything" as much as he wanted, and he complied, trying to bring back strength and rebuild the muscle tissues lost during the decline of his body. With hard work and determination, Tom slowly regained muscular strength for walking, then moved around for simple tasks in the house. Finally after many months he became strong enough for general exercise.

There were also psychological barriers Tom had to fight through. It was disconcerting to have no memory of the cardiac arrest, or of the preceding four months—to suddenly just find himself in a severely weakened physical state with no historical "hooks" to hang the experience on. He had to rely on others' first-hand reports of what had happened to him. It was three months before he drove the car for the first time. Others may not remember this arduous journey because they didn't live it. Tom realizes the miracle, though. Every day his prayers begin with, "Thank you, God, for this miracle day."

Remembering this miracle experience bolsters my faith for all things. Hopeless things are never truly hopeless. God is the God over the Impossible. All things are possible with God.

That truth is stamped indelibly in my spirit. Permanently. It is a reference point my mind returns to as new issues arise in prayer. I remember it, I review it, and my faith is revitalized as I do.

Obviously, the touch of God for Tom's miraculous return to life and healing was awesome and life-changing for us in every sense of the word. But that miracle event was a particular point on the continuum of many more events. That was then; this is now; and "life goes on." But life goes on with heightened awareness that our lives are finite, and every day counts. We are energized by a need to become and do whatever we believe our God has in mind for us. "Whatever you do, do heartily as unto the Lord," Tom often quotes to remind himself and others that our days have purpose and opportunities we don't want to miss.

"Whatever you do, do your work heartily, as for the Lord rather than for men, knowing that from the Lord you will receive the reward of the inheritance. It is the Lord Christ whom you serve"(Colossians 3:23-24).

Had our spiritual lives not been touched by the miracle, the physical "life going on" might have resumed a normal flow as before, as soon as Tom's strength returned. This is our personal modern-day example of the truth Pat recognized and spoke about, "Miracles are soon forgotten. It is the living God we need to have our eyes on, not the miracle."

In some important ways, remembering Pat's illness and passing has had as much significant, long-lasting impact on my faith as the miracle of Tom's restored life. Comparing the experiences, there are many similarities in the two stories. Both experiences were profound in developing and shaping faith, even though the physical outcomes were entirely different. Many times I have remembered Pat's insistence that we look not for a miracle, but that we look for God Himself. Although we loved God already, during the soul-trying times of Pat's illness we experienced a deep solidifying of our faith.

After his passing, I learned just how profoundly my relationship with Jesus had developed during that time. It came into view vividly one morning, years later. I was sitting at the patio table with a cup of coffee, my Bible, and my journal. I had just read a conversation Jesus had with His disciples when many of His followers gave up their faith in Him and went back to "life as usual."

"From this time many of his disciples turned back and no longer followed him. 'You do not want to leave too, do you?' Jesus asked the Twelve. Simon Peter answered him, 'Lord, to whom shall we go? You have the words of eternal life. We have come to

believe and to know that you are the Holy One of
God'" (John 6:66-69 NIV).

I closed my Bible and opened my journal. Writing my thoughts, which often turned to prayers, helped me think more carefully about issues I was trying to sort out. I had been a widow for eight years. I was missing Pat desperately and wondering if I would ever have another life partner. I wrote in my journal:

"As I prayed this morning, I began to imagine my loved ones, one at a time, sitting at the table with me. I pictured the first one seated in a chair next to me, and I placed Jesus in another chair with us. Here we three sat in this happy hypothetical time, sipping lemonade and conversing together on a beautiful sunny day. I asked myself, 'If I had to choose between these two for a life-long companion, who would it be?' I repeated this imaginary pairing with each loved one, seating them one by one between Jesus and me. Each time I asked myself, 'Who do I choose, if I have to choose between these two?' It has to be Jesus. When I imagine Jesus being sent away, I cannot bear the thought. I can live without a loved one, as precious as he or she is to my heart, because

Jesus will help me through that desolation. I have learned this during these years without Pat. Jesus knows my every heartache and understands me when no one else does. He provides for me and gives me wise guidance. He is able to fill me up in my spirit to help me live without Pat. But no one could help me live without Jesus. He is everything. When I imagine only Jesus at the table with me, He is more than enough, even in the absence of any other beloved family member or friend! What a revelation! I wouldn't know this if I hadn't had to say good-bye to Pat and my other sweet loved ones. The best part is those good-byes are only temporary. One day I'll see them in heaven, and today is only a temporary separation. Thank You, Lord, that I never have to say 'Good-bye' to You!"

We are meant to remember the blessings God delivers to us, whether they are external visible blessings, or invisible blessings of transformed attitudes, or answered prayers we've prayed for ourselves and others. As I recalled the countless times I had received comfort, wisdom, and guidance, my faith was refreshed. I learned that believing and trusting God really meant more to me than anything else in life. This strengthened my faith and eased my loneliness.

God Remembers

The Bible is full of God telling His people, "I will remember...":

Genesis 8:1 *"But God **remembered** Noah..."*

Exodus 2:24 *"...and God **remembered** His covenant with Abraham, Isaac, and Jacob."*

I Samuel 1:19 *"...and the LORD **remembered** her."*

God remembers us. He remembers what He has said to us. He remembers His promises to us. He remembers His covenants. God values relationship. Just as He remembers us, He is pleased when we remember Him and His goodness. Remembering is a gift we give to others; and it is a gift to God when we remember Him. It also is a gift we give ourselves when we remember how God has helped us. Remembering fortifies our faith for present trials.

David responded to a crisis by *"encouraging himself in the LORD His God"* (I Samuel 30:6) (KJV). The New American Standard Bible translates the words "encouraged himself" to "strengthened himself." Encouraging is strengthening. It was an action he took upon himself. Sometimes we have to encourage ourselves when there is nobody else who will do it. How did David do it? He encouraged himself "in the Lord His God." Not an impersonal, unknown god. *"His* God." His personal relationship with God and experiences of God's power in the past encouraged him for his present need.

We encourage ourselves in the Lord and strengthen our faith when we intentionally remember His faithfulness to us. Focusing on how He has come through for us in past times gives us confidence that He will come through again. Promises in His Word will be true today just as other promises have been true for us in former times. We remember the ways He has shown Himself strong on our behalf. We deliberately enter our mental storehouse of experiences, answered prayers, and blessings, and remember what is true about God. *We choose to remember that God remembers us.*

> *"And David was greatly distressed; for the people spoke of stoning him, because the soul of all the people was grieved, every man for his sons and for his daughters: but David* **encouraged himself** *in the LORD his God"* (1 Samuel 30:6 KJV). In NASB, *"strengthened himself in the Lord His God."*

David had practiced this valuable lesson before. As a very young man, he confronted the giant warrior, Goliath, confidently remembering how God had helped him in dangerous times while he shepherded his father's sheep. Remembering how God had kept him from harm and had

enabled him to kill wild animals that attacked the sheep, David
had no doubt God also would be with him for hand-to-hand
combat with Goliath.

*"David said to Saul, 'Your servant was tending his
father's sheep. When a lion or a bear came and took a
lamb from the flock, I went out after him and attacked
him, and rescued it from his mouth; and when he rose
up against me, I seized him by his beard and struck him
and killed him. Your servant has killed both the lion and
the bear; and this uncircumcised Philistine will be like
one of them, since he has taunted the armies of the living
God." And David said, 'The Lord who delivered me
from the paw of the lion and from the paw of the bear,
He will deliver me from the hand of this Philistine"*
(1Samuel 17:34-37).

This well-known story has a satisfying ending that is
often referred to in secular conversation and literature. It is a
thrilling story of faith and courage rewarded. The size of the
threat wasn't equal to the God-empowered faith of a young
man who remembered God's help from previous times and
counted on it for his present need.

The theme of remembering recurs over and over in the
Bible. God knows we have a tendency to get caught up in the

distractions and busyness of our days, but we need to take time to sit down, be quiet, and remember. We can feel overwhelmed when we are in the middle of conflict and have problems to solve. Our loving, compassionate God tells us He is gracious, compassionate, powerful, and available. He tells us to remember these things, and be strengthened.

*"He has made His wonders to be **remembered**; The LORD is gracious and compassionate"* (Psalm 11:4).

*You shall **remember** that you were a slave in the land of Egypt, and the LORD your God brought you out of there by a mighty hand and by an outstretched arm..."* (Deuteronomy 5:15).

*"So these days were to be **remembered** and celebrated throughout every generation, every family, every province and every city; and these days of Purim were not to fail from among the Jews, or their memory fade from their descendants"* (Esther 9:28).

*"All the ends of the earth will **remember** and turn to the Lord", and all the families of the nations will worship before You."* (Psalms 22:27).

*"I will **remember** my song in the night; I will meditate with my heart..."* (Psalms 77:6).

*"I shall **remember** the deeds of the Lord; Surely I will **remember** Your wonders of old." I will meditate on all Your work And muse on Your deeds. Your way, O God, is holy; What god is great like our God? You are the God who works wonders; You have made known Your strength among the peoples. You have by Your power redeemed Your people, the sons of Jacob and Joseph. Selah"* (Psalm 77:11-15).

*"And they **remembered** that God was their rock, And the Most High God their Redeemer"*(Psalms 78:35).

*"**Remember** His wonders which He has done, His marvels and the judgments uttered by His mouth..."* (Psalms 105:5).

Forgetting

Not only can we choose to remember God's help for us in times past, we can wisely choose to forget things that hinder us in times present. Some major hindrances to faith are wrong ideas we tell ourselves about God. We can become stuck in wrong attitudes, rather than moving forward in faith. Wrong attitudes may be identified by our self-talk; or they may be lying dormant in a dark corner of our minds where they remain undetected, buried under fear, discouragement, or regret. We don't always recognize what's hindering our faith.

Peel off the layers and it may sound like:

"God is mad at me."

"I don't deserve to ask for anything."

"God has more important things/people to deal with than with me."

"I can't expect God to forgive me."

"I can't forgive myself."

"I'm too far away from God for Him to hear me."

"I really blew it again. God is too disappointed in me to help me now."

All of the above statements are shown to be untrue of God's character when we read the Bible. The Scriptures are replete with affirmations that none of us is so far from God that we cannot receive His forgiveness and His welcoming arms. The story Jesus told of the prodigal son is a stunning example not only of the repentant son, but also of the loving father who waited for his erring son to return home. Believing what God says in His Word, we must forget our past failings and the self-talk that accompanies them, and run back into the arms of our loving Father. This is a rewarding study—about God's lavish forgiveness for all our sins and His outstretched arms to His sorrowful children who seek reconciliation. He never refuses a request for forgiveness. Our task is to accept

His forgiveness, believe it, and forget the past. This is not always easy. But God shows us the way by His holy example.

God forgets

God tells the prophet Jeremiah that not only will He forgive iniquity, He will remember their sin *no more*. God *decides* to forget it. Forever. God, who has a perfect memory, chooses *not* to remember. Ever.

> *"...they will all know Me, from the least of them*
> *to the greatest of them," declares the LORD, "for*
> *I will forgive their iniquity, and their sin I will*
> *remember no more" (Jeremiah 31:34).*

The psalmist repeats this theme. Inspired by God, he sings a song of God's great lovingkindness, telling that the Lord has compassion on us, like a father has compassion on his children. Grudges are not held. Bitterness is non-existent. No nagging. No "I told you so." Just forgiveness and a throwing away of the failings, sins, transgressions so far that they cannot be seen, heard, measured, or reviewed. As far as the east is from the west. East never meets west in this expansive, immeasurable universe.

> *"For as high as the heavens are above the earth,*
> *So great is His lovingkindness toward those who fear*
> *Him.*

As far as the east is from the west,

So far has He removed our transgressions from us.

Just as a father has compassion on his children,

So the Lord has compassion on those who fear Him"

(Psalms 103:11-13).

The apostle Paul spoke of his own need to forget past things which would impede his progress in living a life of faith.

> *"...but one thing I do: forgetting what lies behind*
> *and reaching forward to what lies ahead, I press*
> *on toward the goal for the prize of the upward call*
> *of God in Christ Jesus"* (Philippians 3:13-14).

Paul confessed being in a process, not yet having reached the pinnacle of faith he was reaching for. He stated his goal, *"to know Him [Christ] and the power of His resurrection,"* to become more like Jesus, more surrendered to the will of God. Paul recognized that what he had previously done and thought was achievement would prove worthless in eternity. With all this in mind, Paul wrote, *"forgetting what lies behind..."*

God declared to us His intention to forget every forgiven sin. Paul knew this and declared his resolution to also forget his own past failings and self-righteousness. He is our example for using forgetfulness in an empowering way.

Remembering to forget

When we intentionally remember the promises of God, we have opportunities to see God work in new ways, ways we have never dreamed of. Even our best experiences so far do not predict the surprises God has in store for our futures when we encourage ourselves, remember what He has done, and remember what He has told us in His Word. It's time to remember.

When we intentionally forget the things that hinder our faith, we are released for new possibilities and freedom from past failings. We are forgiven for every slip-up, every fall, every doubt, every offense, as soon as we bring it to God and ask for His forgiveness. Receiving His forgiveness, we can deliberately choose to agree with Him to *forget* our past sins, doubt, and unbelief. Then we are able to move forward in faith. We are no longer burdened by the "what if's" and "if only's." Our feet are free to run on the faith road, with freedom to enjoy God's next step for us. It's time to forget.

King Solomon, historically noted for his wisdom, wrote in Ecclesiastes,

> *"There is an appointed time for everything. And there is a time for every event under heaven—* (Ecclesiastes 3:1)... *"A time to search and a time*

to give up as lost; A time to keep and a time to throw away" (Ecclesiastes 3:6).

It's valuable to take time to remember our significant events and reflect on how they have shaped our faith. Our faith will come out either stunted or strengthened according to where we focus our attention.

There is a time to remember and a time to forget.

Chapter 11

More Precious than Gold

Although we long for a quiet and undisturbed life, we will meet trials and upheaval along the way. Some come as a result of our own mistakes, wrong decisions, or short-sightedness. Some come through other people who don't see things the same way we do and misunderstand or resent us. Some come as persecution for our Christian beliefs and evidences of our faith. Some come from natural forces of the world, like earthquakes, fires, or floods. Some come from Satan's attempts to thwart the work of God in us. We will have trials. But there is good news. Although we live in a world fraught with emotional baggage, evil, and metaphorical landmines,

God takes notice of every challenge we face and He is not stymied or dismayed. He knows how to turn our struggles into a stunning performance of His grace and it is His delight to do so.

Many years ago, I learned that God powerfully overrules in trials that would otherwise destroy me. In the earliest years of my new life in Christ, a very tragic accident occurred that impacted our family and our faith. In spite of the horror, I vividly recall the amazing ways God demonstrated His intimate presence with us. It began the night before. I was reading the Bible with awe and basking in the wonder of God's love. My spirit felt filled to overflowing. I remember being deeply touched by the sense of God's provision and I wept with joy that I actually held in my hands the very words of the eternal God. Giving me this profound reverence and assurance of God's nearness, the Holy Spirit was preparing me for events that would unfold the next day.

When I learned the devastating news eighteen hours later, I was overwhelmed with sorrow for the victims and all those involved in the tragedy. My broken heart spilled out its shattered pieces with sobs, "How could this happen?" The description "the bottom dropped out" was suddenly a dreadful reality to me. But very present with my intense grief was the same powerful sense I had felt the night before when I wrapped my arms around my Bible and hugged it tightly, thanking God for such an extraordinary Gift. God had impressed upon me that my preservation and sustenance would always come through His Word, no matter what the circumstance. That proved to be the case. His Word was my stability.

Wounded, but knowing where my comfort would come from, I ran to His Word as often as I could during breaks in the days' necessary routines of tending to children, cooking, washing clothes, and other mundane tasks. I remember the surprising sensation of being in a protective bubble—a bubble filled with peace, security, and a certainty that God had not deserted us. I know this fortification came from God's unchanging Truth filled with promises that He would bring us through.

These scriptures will always be precious to me because of how powerfully they spoke to me at a time of desperate need. I have returned to them many times to soak up the comfort and reassurance they provide. I have never been disappointed in their power to calm my fears and to rearrange my attitudes.

"Cast thy burden upon the Lord, and he shall sustain thee; he shall never suffer the righteous to be moved" (Psalms 55:22 KJV).

"Be merciful unto me, O God, be merciful unto me: for my soul trusts in thee. Yea, in the shadow of thy wings will

I make my refuge, until these calamities be passed by. I will cry unto God most high; unto God who performs all things for me. He shall send from heaven, and save me from the reproach of him that would swallow me up. Selah. God shall send forth his mercy and his truth" (Psalm 57:1-3 KJV).

Trials are for transformation. Regardless of the origin of our trials, God is pleased to take the worst times of our lives and use them in amazing ways to transform us and enrich our relationship with Him. As we look to Him, He turns cursing into blessing. Peter, Christ's disciple and writer of I Peter and II Peter, could speak to this out of his own experience and that of fellow believers who were being persecuted for following Jesus.

"That the trial of your faith, being much more precious than gold that perishes, though it be tried by fire, might be found unto praise and honor and glory at the appearing of Jesus Christ" (I Peter 1:7 KJV).

"Beloved, think it not strange concerning the fiery trial which is to try you, as though some strange thing happened to you; But rejoice, inasmuch as ye are partakers of Christ's sufferings; that, when his glory

shall be revealed, ye may be glad also with exceeding joy" (I Peter 4:12).

What a word picture is recorded in I Peter! Peter first acknowledges that we are "Beloved," a word which speaks of the love of God for us. With that established, the fact that we will experience trials, great trials, hot trials, is placed into context. Our trials are not to be interpreted as a lack of God's love for us. Even though we are beloved children of God, we will experience fierce trials. The word used for "furnace" in Proverbs 27:21, *"the furnace for gold,"* and the word Peter used for "fiery trials" come from the same word meaning "a burning." This word also appears in Psalm 66, referring to the refining process for silver. It is clear the burning in each case refers to the smelting process. *"For thou, O God, hast proved us; thou hast tried us as silver is tried"* (Psalm   66:10).

Like the refining of silver and gold, these are not pointless, haphazard trials; they are trials meant for our good, to strengthen our faith. The word that was translated "tried", "proved," or" tested" means to test something for the purpose of approving it. The idea is refining faith so that it becomes pure and lustrous like gold and shines as a testimony to the power and all-sufficiency of our Savior. *"The genuineness of your faith,"* as the NIV translation says, is *"more precious than gold that perishes."* Earthly gold, though admired for its beauty and hoarded for its value, is merely a mineral extracted from the earth, is finite, and subject to decay and destruction. Faith is much more precious to God than the shiny element so valued by the world. Because of His high esteem for faith and His tender love for us, His children, God works to increase and polish our faith for His glory and our enrichment.

The picturesque phrasing in I Peter elicits the image of a goldsmith standing over a refining pot that is used to obtain the precious metal. Gold requires extreme heat to force the impurities from the ore. The refiner must progressively intensify the heat to liquefy the metal. Finally the elements separate, and the impurities rise to the surface. The workman then carefully skims the impurities from the surface of the molten gold and increases the heat for repeated steps. At the same time, the refiner is studiously observing the liquid treasure in the crucible. He knows the gold has been made pure when he can see his reflection mirrored on the surface of the liquid gold.

Suffering is the crucible for the Christian. Trials of illness, hardships, disappointments, losses, persecution, even temptations from Satan are used by God to turn up the heat in order to extract shining faith from His beloved children. As a perfectly loving Father, He watches the process intently. It is God's desire that the trial of our faith *"be found to praise and glory and honor."* With greatest attention, He scrutinizes every flicker of the blazing fire, limiting the intensity to just what is needed, no more. With care, He skims off the impurities—those things we have allowed through complacency or self-sufficiency or unbelief or blindness. The process is repeated until with great pleasure and joy He sees in His precious child the reflection of the face of His Beloved Son.

These tests or trials are not to punish us for our failings, for He loves us dearly. He made us, knows our weaknesses, and is compassionately mindful that we need Him to hold us together when life is crumbling around us.

"Like a father pities his children, so Jehovah pities them that fear Him. For He   knows our frame; He remembers that we are dust" (Psalms 103:13-14).

The dust is what we are made of, but this statement is not a put-down; it is a reminder that God knows our present limitations and fledgling faith, and He will not allow more than we can bear. In times of severe trials, I confess I have questioned that premise, feeling something *was* too much to bear. But God's Word reminded me I was not asked to bear it alone. Jesus is our burden bearer and offers His aid. He said,

"Come unto Me, all ye who are weary and burdened. Take my yoke upon you, and learn of Me, for I am

gentle and humble in heart, and you will find rest for your souls. For my yoke is easy and my burden is light" (Matthew 11:28-30 NIV).

A heavy burden weighing upon our shoulders is not easy or light. So Jesus invites us to cast our burdens on Him, and allow Him to share the weight of it, as we yoke ourselves together with Him. Sharing the yoke, Jesus will carry as much of that burden as I cannot bear. And while He bears the burden along with me, side-by-side, I get to know Him better. God has given us every provision we need to help us grow in our faith-walk, inner peace, and confidence as we give Him greater room in our lives.

"Jehovah thy God is in the midst of thee, a mighty one who will save; he will rejoice over thee with joy; he will rest in his love; he will joy over thee with singing" (Zephaniah 3:17 ASV).

I am amazed that God sings. I shouldn't be, because He created music, made the angels, gave them their songs; and singing is often referred to in the Bible when we read about angels and heaven. It's just that I never imagined *God* singing. Even more amazing to me is that God sings over *us*. What a heart-stirring thought—that we bring pleasure to God, and to such a degree that He sings with joy!

I am growing in my appreciation for God's everlasting great love. I am buoyed up when I reflect on His "Father" attributes of guidance, protection, instruction, and discipline; and especially the Abba "Daddy" attributes of intimacy, playfulness, affection. A "Daddy" delights in his children.

Through fiery trials of serial bad news and multiple losses, I admit I felt the scorching heat of the refining blaze and at times thought surely I would be consumed. I didn't have any sense of being "my Daddy's delight." Sometimes I had to fight for faith. Waiting for emotional restoration after the battles was as trying as the trials themselves. With all my might, I clung to Scriptures like Isaiah 61:3 (NIV):

"He provides for those who grieve in Zion— to bestow on them a crown of beauty instead of ashes, the oil of joy instead of mourning, and a garment of praise instead of a spirit of despair. They will be called oaks of righteousness, a planting of the Lord for the display of his splendor,"

While I was in the fire, and blow fell upon blow, I wondered if I would be the one exception who would be denied such blessings. However, deep in my heart, I held onto what I had determined earlier to be unalterable Truth. Things were in disarray, but I resolved to trust that my time in the furnace would one day bring me forth as gold. This kept the pieces of my life from flying apart, and of course I did not become "the one exception."

God is faithful and plays no favorites. In fact, the truth stated in Hebrews 12 is that God's children will be allowed to experience discipline and will suffer trying times, just as loving earthly parents must sometimes allow their children to suffer through things that will build character and later be invaluable to them.

Inherent in the word translated "discipline" are two other words—correction and guidance.[1] God's purpose is not to ruin us, but to guide and strengthen us, *"afterwards yielding the peaceable fruit of righteousness"* (Hebrews 12:11). I have seen this result in my own life as the fires cooled down and a newly-forged mettle emerged. Patience, long-suffering, and self-control, in particular, have shown up in greater strength.

As a young Christian, before I had learned very much about the Bible, I was introduced to a passage that set the stage for my faith journey. It is familiar to many Christians and is a source of comfort and encouragement during trying times.

"For we know that God works all things together for good to them who love Him and are the called according to His purpose" (Romans 8:28). (NIV)

Reading this, I began to put it into practice. I determined to thank God for everything, even the trials, because I believed what it said, that God would work it all together for good. It became a bit of an objective experiment in faith. I kept a little spiral notebook and wrote down various circumstances, praying over them, and thanking God that even though it looked like a regrettable event, somehow He would work things together for good. Then I made notes about the developments in these circumstances.

It was a wonderful experience. Time after time, I saw amazing demonstrations of unexpected good coming forth, and excitedly wrote the processes and final outcomes that proved to me forever that this Biblical statement is not baseless optimism. It is God's declaration of His intentions for us. He wants that "good" to always be our expectation of Him. My Romans 8:28 "Record of Good Outcomes" included blessings from things like having our living room ceiling falling down and then receiving a no-cost-to-us improvement; seeing God provide many times when our monthly budget couldn't; running out of gas in a very timely way and place; and seeing people come to know Jesus through a dreadful tragedy. Whether it is a physical trial, monetary, relational, psychological, or any other kind, God wants us to know that no situation is hopeless. He provides solutions that will surprise and delight us. He only asks us to exercise our faith.

"There is no temptation taken you, but such is common to man; But God is faithful, who will not permit you to be tempted beyond what you are able, but will with the temptation make a way of escape that you may be able to bear it" (I Corinthians 10:13 KJV).

I thank God that He began teaching me these surprising lessons early on, because through the years they have been my anchors during stormy seasons, and my delight during sunshiny days. I want to be more like Jesus; I want to please my Father. Discovering that trials are opportunities to draw closer to His heart makes them worth the pain. Thinking of Him singing over me, even as I wait for His ultimate rescue, is beyond joy.

Chapter 12

Joy and Peace in Believing

Believing for a miracle, having a settled, unshakable faith for it, and yet not seeing it come to pass is surely among the most emotional and difficult experiences to work through. To believe, have no doubt, and to wait expectantly for a glorious outcome, then see the final outcome shockingly unlike what was expected is devastating. Such an event is like a tectonic shift, a gargantuan upheaval to the faith that waited for it.

I know—I have been there. For months after Pat died, it was agonizing to me to hear about God's miraculous interventions in other's lives. While I was thrilled at the grace and power of God operating for them, my own lack of receiving that same kind of answer ricocheted against my ragged emotions for a long time.

What *happened*? Why not me? Does God play favorites? Did I not have enough faith? Did I not hear God's still small voice when I thought I had? Can I even *hear* God? Does God hear *me*? were frequent reverberations in my mind.

These are questions to wrestle with when faith is confronted with unexpected outcomes. And it *is* a wrestling match. Satan takes advantage of such upheaval, and attempts to accentuate our doubts, pain, and sense of alienation from God. A relentless enemy, he will suggest all kinds of malicious lies to our wounded hearts: *You're not as important to God as these others are. You didn't have enough faith. God betrayed you. God doesn't care. You wasted a lot of time and energy reading your Bible and praying. You embarrassed yourself by speaking words of faith, telling others you were believing God for a miracle. You don't know God like you think you do.* Satan is the father of lies. We must never forget that. He plays on our weaknesses, our woundedness. His objective is always the same, to destroy faith and wreak havoc in our lives any way he can.

The wrestling match takes place in our minds and our emotions, not in our spirits. It starts with wrong thoughts. Unchecked, these lead to wrong emotions. It's helpful to realize Satan has no access to our spirit-man. The most he can do to my inner self is to infiltrate my thinking through others' misguided words or my own thoughts. This causes a devoted Christian some confusion. While I knew that I believed in God, that He is the one and only Most High God, perfect in all His ways, worthy of praise and worship, my mind and emotions were being bombarded by thoughts I knew I did not believe, knew were wrong.

It was a relief when I learned that those unwanted thoughts were not generated by me, but were from a subtle, wicked source. The Bible speaks of the weapons of our warfare being of the spirit, and *"mighty to the pulling down of strongholds and every high thing that exalts itself against the knowledge of God and bringing into captivity every thought to the obedience of Christ"* (II Corinthians 10:4-5).

Strongholds come first as subtle questions, similar to the one in the Garden of Eden—"Did God really say...? They slyly infiltrate our thoughts and if they meet no resistance they can become entrenched as a stronghold. The mental battle is implied by the words "against the *knowledge*" and "every *thought*." When I read about this, it was illuminating and explained the ideas that were battering my mind—ideas contrary to what I actually believed. I was involved in mental warfare!

The Bible says we have *"the shield of faith by which we can quench all the fiery darts of the enemy"* (Ephesians 6:16). So I held up the shield of faith against the doubts, lies, and accusations, reminding myself that God was with me, and spoke aloud what God declares in His Word. *"I will not, I will not, I*

will not ever leave you or forsake you" (Hebrews 13:5).
(Kenneth Wuest translates from the Greek in his New
Testament Expanded Translation[1] and supplies this triple
repetition to communicate the intended emphasis in the original
words.) God is with me. His Word is true. I am never left alone.

During the time following the discovery of Pat's seriously
compromised heart, it was natural for us to draw close to God.
We recognized Him as our source for all things and our faithful
provider. There were many, many times we saw Him work
wonderfully to encourage us, and our encouragement spilled
over in conversations to tell others about Jesus. We were
confident that He was with us every step of the way. Because of
books we were reading, personal Bible study, and prayer, we
felt assurance that God would miraculously heal Pat for a
glorious testimony of His power and love. Even when the
medical reports became less encouraging, we believed we
would see a miracle healing.

There were some unusual occurrences that fueled our faith.
Timely messages from different sources, and surprising signs
that were beyond coincidental and could not be explained by
human reason or natural causes. What was most meaningful to
us was the powerful peace that reigned in our hearts, an anchor
of comfort in the midst of tumultuous events and circumstances.

Why would God allow us to believe so firmly that He was
about to bring a miracle of healing? Was it from God? Or was it

our denial? Or just wishful thinking, as some must have privately thought about us? Periodically, I have raised these questions to God in times of quiet reading and contemplation of His Word. The Lord says, *"Seek me and ye shall surely find me if ye search for me with all your heart"* (Jeremiah 29:13). I believe the answers are in Hebrews, chapters 11 and 12, a portion of the Bible that deals with the weighty issue of mighty faith, even among those who did not live to see the promise, but who persevered with faith-filled expectation. *"These died in faith,"* the Bible states. They died while they were still believing with faith, waiting for the promise.

Key to accepting this is remembering that our life on planet earth is only temporary. Living here, all our senses tell us this is the *real* reality. After all, I can see, hear, touch, taste, and smell it. It's very easy to forget there is a spiritual reality beyond our senses. The greater reality is eternal, the unseen and very real world that already exists and awaits us in heaven, with rewards that we haven't seen unfold during our lifetime.

This is not merely optimistic speculation. The inspired writer of Hebrews 12 speaks of this "far off country" and names it as our true home, a place not built by human hands. The challenge to us now is to trust God's Word, and view that future home as the ultimate destination we are journeying toward while our feet are on this foreign soil. The Bible calls us "citizens of heaven," for that is where we are already spiritually dwelling as joint heirs with Christ and are going to dwell for eternity. *"God raised us up with Christ and seated us with him in the heavenly realms in Christ Jesus"* (Ephesians 2:6. NIV). It is in that direction the saints in Hebrews 12:2 have their attention riveted, their eyes looking, their feet pointed. And their faith rewarded.

For years, Hebrews chapter 12 bothered me when I read it. I couldn't grasp the meaning for the saints who were sawn asunder, stoned, martyred, were treated as the off-scouring of the earth, and died without reward. What they endured here on earth seems unimaginably horrible. They died without receiving what God had promised them and which they absolutely believed God would fulfill. Is that fair?

Yes, if we remember that it isn't over when we die. For those of us who believe on Christ, our lives are simply transferred from one place of residence to a new one. God's promises still stand to be fulfilled; they don't reach an expiration date. They follow us to our new location.

Several friends had tried to comfort me with, "God did answer your prayer, Marilee. He healed Pat in heaven." This was no comfort to me. I felt it was a cop-out. My prayer had been that Pat would be healed now, on earth, for the glory of God, because that healing could not take place without the supernatural interventional power of God. *That* prayer was not answered. At the time I had a picture of how God would get the glory from a miraculous healing seen by many here on earth, just as when Lazarus was raised from the dead. Many believed on Jesus as a result. So many, in fact, that the Pharisees conspired to put Lazarus to death, because his life was undeniable evidence of the resurrection-working power of Jesus Christ. I had my idea of how things should work to give God glory. However, my ideas are limited by finite understanding. God's thoughts are not like my thoughts. His thoughts are higher than my thoughts. His ways are higher and greater than my ways. He knows what He is doing and why.

Now I realize my friends were closer to being right than I was. Some of those mentioned in Hebrews chapter 11 died without receiving the promise they were expecting. Over time, I have begun to realize that their faith is not a problem in the Bible. It is an amazing example of authentic faith, believing God at all costs.

"These all, although they had witness borne to them through their faith, did not receive the promise, God having provided some better thing for us, in order that they without us should not be brought to completeness" (Hebrews 11:39-40 KJV).

"These all, although they had witness borne to them through their faith...," This is our experience, too. There are times we feel a strong inner witness that something is meant to happen. It is energized by faith. There is no human

explanation for such an impression, but it is very present and is sustained over an extended period, against reason or logic. Sometimes it comes to pass; other times it does not.

Like those spoken of in this chapter, we may not receive the promise that our faith so strongly witnesses to us. This does not necessarily mean we were wrong to believe it, even though it doesn't come to pass. If God gives us faith for something, He has a reason for us to cling to that faith without wavering. Faith sustains us in times that no emotion or resolve can. *"You have seen and now you believe. Blessed are those who have **not** seen and yet believe,"* Jesus told Thomas (John 20:29). Skeptics will say that this is blind faith. Not according to Jesus. He says this is blessed faith.

The second part of the verse *"...in order that they without us should not be brought to completeness"* is a reminder that we believers are all in this together, bound together by the life of Christ—God's people, one in the Spirit, in unity with Him, not separate from one another, all making up the Body of Christ. Jesus prayed, *"That they all may be one, as You, Father, are in Me, and I in You, that they also may be one in Us, so that the world may believe that You sent Me"* (John 17:21).

"Brought to completeness" or "brought to perfection," as it is also translated in some Bible versions, means coming into "full development, growth into maturity in godliness."

On a quick reading it sounds as if they might not be brought to completeness if it weren't for us. That is not the idea. We, "us," are included in the thought that we are all brought to completeness in the same way, together, not that there are two or more separate groups being brought to completion. The distinction is that while they have completed their journey here, we are still on the path and are still required to walk with faith. They now have finished the race, having completed their journey of faith. We, however, are still *"seeing through a glass darkly, while they are seeing face to face"* (1 Corinthians 13:12).

The emphasis is on *"God having provided some better thing for us."* That "better thing" is yet to be revealed when we will join those who have preceded us. Certainly it includes many facets of God's grace through the finished work of Christ, and I believe there may be another aspect of the "better thing." While we are still in the race, our faith is in process. Our faith is being helped to "come to completeness" and is being refined by our present difficulties as we consider their example and are inspired to walk by faith as they did. Their steadfast faith is our example. God gave them grace to endure and remain faithful during their lifetimes. We, learning from their example, also are able to see beyond our present trials, and are inspired to keep our focus on the heavenly country during our lifetimes. We, then, are partakers with them in the walk of faith, trusting God to fulfill His promises, whether today or tomorrow, and even beyond what we see with our limited vision.

In the same way, those who come after us will be helped by our examples of living by faith, tenaciously clinging to the Truth God has given us in His Word, whether we see tangible, "today" results, or not. In God's view, everything from beginning to end is one fabulous panorama, not the pieces we see and become fixated on with our limited view. We all, as members of the Body of Christ, are brought to completion together, as God's grand plan of the ages is worked out, generation by generation, and individual by individual. We are part of a plan that is far more magnificent than just our here and now.

But we live in the here and now. And in our here and now we are helped by remembering God cannot fail, and every promise is *"Yes and Amen" in Christ Jesus"* (2 Corinthians 1:20). There is much comfort in patiently waiting for what is sure to come, even if it is delayed.

The faith we had that Pat would be healed on this earth was a glorious time of anticipation and worship. Hope is a healing and strengthening force.

"Now the God of hope fill you with all joy and peace in believing, that you may abound in hope through the power of the Holy Spirit" (Romans 15:13).

We needed the God of hope, and He was there. There were many trying and scary moments in the time we waited for God to heal. There were times of confusion and anguish. But there were also many joyous moments of peace and songs in the night when hope soared in the face of grim medical news.

Because of this God-given hope, lives were touched. We spoke to doctors and nurses in the University of Utah Medical Center's Heart Transplant Unit, and some gave their hearts to Christ, not because we were believing God for a miracle, but because they could see the hope, stability, and peace we were experiencing during the two years of tests, consultations, and emergency interventions. Pat calmly told them, "I'm not afraid of dying. I know where I'm going. I have put my faith in Jesus Christ and He is sustaining me." His demeanor was visible evidence of the power and stability in his life, and God gave us opportunities to tell others more about the love of God and His gift of eternal life through His Son Jesus.

Pat's heart continued to weaken, but his spirit expanded in its capacity to love and worship God and to tell others how wonderfully God works. He took every opportunity to talk about God's love and provision through Jesus Christ, and to encourage and pray with others. I often heard him express, "God is a God of miracles. But miracles are soon forgotten. We need to focus on God Himself, not the miracles. He is Lord, and He is worthy of our praise, no matter what." To prove his point, he referred to the miracles recorded in the Old Testament, and noted how quickly they were ignored or discounted by God's own people soon after their experiences. David wrote about their short-term memory and cold-heartedness in Psalm 78, chronicling miracles of God in the Israelites' history. And Jesus faced this same reality many times during His ministry, as recorded in the gospels.

When complications removed Pat from the heart transplant list, he was not dismayed. "God can heal me here, or He can heal me there. Either way, I win," was his attitude. That is a powerful witness of faith with eyes looking toward the far-off city described in Hebrews 11:11-16. His witness now is joined with the ones we read about in Hebrews 11:39 and in Hebrews 12:1-2. It is a witness of God's great power, wisdom, provision, and love, rooted in confidence that no detail escapes the eyes or heart of the One who made us, died for us, and guides our steps.

It inspires me to live with that kind of faith—a settled expectation that in our ultimate destination, that heavenly country, everything will be rewarded and fulfilled far beyond what we can ask or imagine.

"These all died dominated by faith, not having received the promises, but having seen them afar off and greeted them, also confessed that they were strangers... upon the earth...But now as the case stands, they are reaching

out in their desires for a better country, that is, a heavenly one, because of which God is not ashamed of them to be surnamed their God, for He prepared for them a city." (Hebrews 11:13-16, Wuest)[2]

"Therefore also, as for us, having so great a cloud of those who are bearing testimony [i.e., the heroes of faith of chapter 11] surrounding us, having put off and away from ourselves once for all every encumbrance and that sin which so deftly and cleverly places itself in an entangling way around us, with patience let us be running the race lying before us, looking off and away to Jesus, the originator and perfecter of this aforementioned faith, who instead of the joy then present with Him endured the Cross, despising the shame, and has sat down at the right hand of the throne of God" (Hebrews 12:1-2, Wuest).[3]

Chapter 13

A Different Kind of Victory

Victory sometimes comes in oddly shaped packages. Sometimes it's an obvious victory and the package has a certificate, medal, or trophy to show for it. Sometimes it's winning a personal battle, such as losing 20 pounds or controlling one's temper, and the package holds a self-congratulatory smile and a confident air. Sometimes it's intangible, and a mystery to onlookers who see peace in the midst of adversity. The package is mysteriously wrapped and will be fully revealed later in a heavenly setting. It is a real and lasting victory, transcending trophies and earthly triumphs. This final category is one God empowers and rewards with His riches in glory.

Given a choice, my preference for a comfortable life would take preeminence. I would be prone to choose an obvious victory with applause and cheers and no pain. Chocolate in the package would be an appreciated bonus. But God highly esteems victories of a different kind and invites us to challenges that have eternal significance. With His grace and strength undergirding us, His Word instructing us, and His Holy Spirit coaching and encouraging us, He gives us opportunities to courageously choose to believe Him no matter what our surrounding circumstances are screaming at us.

"This is the victory that overcomes the world, even our faith" (I John 5:4).

When Pat was diagnosed, it was an emotional explosion that stunned our family. It was entirely unexpected, without hereditary precedent and without the typical risk factors that are listed as possible causes of the condition. He had an active lifestyle in his work and recreation and ate healthy foods. His weight was the same as it had been in high school, a trim 170 pounds. He hadn't smoked or experimented with drugs. An occasional glass of wine or beer was his only use of alcohol. The tests were thorough, and the diagnosis was finally labeled idiopathic cardiomyopathy—a heart dysfunction with an unknown origin. It didn't seem fair.

At the time of that shocking discovery, Pat and I had been married for twenty-seven years, and were enjoying life in beautiful McCall, Idaho, where Pat was a Boise Cascade forester and I was an elementary school teacher. We were active in our church as prayer leaders and were earnestly praying for revival of faith on all levels: individuals, marriages, families, churches, communities, and our nation. Pat's terminal heart disease suddenly reshaped our lives and plans. But our prayer focus intensified.

One Sunday morning I spoke to the church. After telling our small congregation about Pat's physical status, and requesting their prayers, I said, "I'm asking you to pray for us, but I'm also asking you to pray for your own spiritual well-being and others'. We all have diseased hearts and need healing and true revival. God has great things in store for us, if we'll only let go of our own control and follow Him whole-heartedly. I believe that Pat's condition and a revival of all our hearts are somehow mysteriously bound together. I don't understand it, but perhaps it is an object lesson for what our deeper needs really are. We all need healing in our hearts. There are battles to be won. Please pray."

The cardiologist urged Pat to get to Salt Lake City to be seen at the Heart Transplant Unit of University of Utah Medical Center. Thus began monthly and biweekly trips for evaluation and monitoring of his heart. Although complications required that he eventually be removed from the transplant list, it was a God-ordained time frame that offered us choices to either grow closer to God and press on in faith, or to wither in despair and give up.

During this time, I repeatedly heard Pat say, "God's reality is greater than this earthly reality around us. God will use this for His glory." He believed it and lived it as he leaned on God during times of progressive physical struggles. Together with others in the community, we believed God was about to, any day now, bring a miracle of healing that would restore strength and wholeness to his weakening body. And like the Biblical description of life and aging, *"Though our outward man perishes, yet our inward man is renewed day by day"* (II Corinthians 4:16 ASV), Pat's inner life was strengthened through the time he devoted to prayer and Bible study. His convictions remained firm. He often expressed, "It doesn't matter how things look, my eyes are on the living God who controls all things. And God never makes mistakes."

Many months later, a friend called me to tell me some wonderful things God was doing in her family to bring strength and healing to damaged relationships. She told me how God had used Pat's declining health to speak to her about a "willing heart." She said what she was so impressed with is that Pat had a "willing heart" to be used by God and to be submissive and faithful to Him in the midst of heavy trials.

The Lord was using him, she said, to show her she also needed to have such a willing heart. She said, "God is using Pat's heart over and over again to speak to many people about the condition of *their* hearts." God's strength often shows up most noticeably at times of our greatest weakness. As Paul wrote regarding his troubles, *"most gladly therefore will I rather glory in my infirmities, that the power of Christ may rest upon me…for when I am weak, I am strong."* (II Corinthians 12:9-10 KJV)

"Victory" was a recurring word that was impressed upon me during my Bible reading and prayer times as we waited week after week, then month after month, for God to bring healing to Pat. While we were immersed in studying and praying for spiritual revival, we experienced some unusual events. We strongly felt God was showing us that He intended to supernaturally heal Pat to bring glory to God and revival to our community.

There were multiple signs and unusual happenings that some would call coincidences, but they delivered sweet messages of encouragement to us, in amazing timeliness just when our faith felt fragmented and ready to crumble. Repeatedly when I began to doubt, something would come in the mail, or I would hear something on the radio, or see a written message that fortified my faith. It was remarkable how many different events God used to remind us He saw us, knew where we were, and was with us all the way. People in our prayer group and community told us that as they prayed they also felt strong conviction that God's plan was to heal Pat and give him many more years on this earth.

I kept a journal during those two years, and recorded the vacillating emotions, surprises, and strong impressions we received as the days passed. Like a rope tug of war, uncertainty pulled against our confidence and, more than once, seemed to gain ground before faith was revitalized again to overcome the adversary. When dark days of disappointment strained against hope, I recorded my despondency as honestly as I had my exuberance, wanting to have a record of reality, not a sugar-coated version, for future reference. Once, after several particularly trying days, we both began to doubt our spiritual acuity, and I wrote,

"Our devastation at again apparently missing God's will, and His leading, is acutely felt. We feel so inept at prayer and following God's lead that we are insecure regarding this continual seeking of the Lord's way for us. How are we to know what is of Him, what is of us, and what is of the enemy? I have prayed for a discerning spirit in this regard for almost a year. These are heavy, dark, desolate times, physically, mentally, emotionally, spiritually. No one will ever know the depths to which we have gone, the longing of our hearts, and the disappointments in our faith and our hope. Only Jesus knows. Only Jesus and we ourselves. It's an experience that is unique to Pat and me. Only we fully know the awful heat of this refining fire; and enduring these fiery trials together, as one, our lives are forever fused in a new bond. We have learned that it is impossible to judge anyone else's circumstances and responses, that lives go through invisible trials that none of us can know about, except Jesus. May we remember this, and be compassionate and merciful toward others in the same way that we desire to be supported.

"Our prayers are not for Pat's life, alone. They are for the building up of the Body of Christ, for hundreds have believed God with us, and keep on believing and praying. Lord, we have asked You to teach us to pray, and to make us a praying army for Your kingdom. We must see victories in order to learn that prayer is a powerful force—that it is effective, that it is worthy of any time sacrificed for it. We need people to pray for revival, for freedom from the subtle and oppressive chains that hold captive minds, hearts, and lives, for the abundant life which belongs to all who come to Christ."

On days like these, we grasped God's Word and reminded ourselves of what is true about God and what is true about His character. A few days after this journal entry, God brought us out of the pit, and I recorded it, too, in my journal.

"I don't want to forget this wonderful touch from God's heart to ours. Yesterday I was talking to Jerry Summers on the phone about our discouragement, and he prayed specifically that God would send us blessings to encourage us. The next morning, we were extremely discouraged (depressed). Everything seemed to hang so heavily upon us. In extreme distress, I cried, 'Lord, send Pat someone to encourage him! I don't know who he needs, but You do. Please have someone call or stop by.' Not three minutes had passed, when the doorbell rang. With anticipation I opened the door, and when I saw who was there, I burst into tears. It was Pat's brother, Mike, with his daughter, Shannon. Angels on our doorstep. Mike had driven that morning from The Dalles, Oregon to Nampa, Idaho to pick up Shannon at the conclusion of her college year and they were headed home. Spontaneously, they had decided to swing through McCall to see Pat before heading home. Their decision took them 100 miles out of their way and 100 miles deep into our thankful hearts.

"An added blessing was the realization that God had already set things in motion to answer our prayer two hours before I had made my request to Him! Unbeknownst to us, Mike and Shannon were just completing that two-hour drive when I began calling out to God for the help we so desperately needed. Just like in the Bible, *'It will also come to pass that before they call, I will answer; and while they are still speaking, I will hear'* (Isaiah 65:24). Mike and Shannon stayed with us for five hours, had dinner with us, watched a little TV basketball, then headed home. They must have reached their home in Oregon about 3:00 A.M. What a gift they gave us with their journey of love. We were doubly blessed. Blessed by the surprising way God showed He heard and answered our prayer. Blessed by the uplifting time with Mike and Shannon. They were exactly who Pat needed for encouragement."

These kinds of surprises, plus new discoveries in God's Word, were touches from God that lifted our spirits when things felt really dark, and we marveled at each new demonstration of God's power to transform our attitudes and perspectives.

One Sunday morning during his call to prayer, our pastor expressed both his faith and his honest questions. He said, "I don't know why God hasn't healed Pat." After church, I received a phone call from a woman who heard the pastor's remark and felt compelled to tell us her impression.

"Marilee, when I heard Pastor Ron say that, I felt a certainty in my heart that *one* reason God hasn't healed Pat yet is that He is using it to teach us all to pray. We are on our knees, now. Others have said this, too. God is teaching us to pray!" She was excited to report this, and it brought a pleased smile and a "Praise God" response when I shared it with Pat.

Our greatest blessing was the certainty of God's presence we felt on most days, and we reveled in the supernatural peace that sometimes enveloped us like a warm blanket on a cold night. I especially loved the songs that I awakened with. Many mornings, even before my eyes opened, my spirit was already singing praises to God. I wondered how the songs could be there, melodies and words, so fresh in my mind. It was as though I had been singing them throughout the night while I slept. I treasured this gift from the Holy Spirit, "who giveth songs in the night" (Job 35:10). There is something supernatural about songs of praise that bring comfort and joy into the soul on a scale nothing can match.

So, what are we to think when our faith has been bolstered to believe God for specific things, and we pray in faith and in the name of Jesus, yet we do not see what we believed would come to pass?

The apostle John wrote of victory that overcomes all things. The victory is wrapped in faith: *"This is the victory that has overcome the world—our faith"* (I John 5:4). This certainly was our experience as we worked through the trials that came. Spiritual steps and stumbles jostled each other for primacy, but Pat delved more deeply into the Word of God, determined that faith would win out. I was inspired by his steady patience and tenacity. He kept a journal, recording insights from the scriptures, favorite songs and hymns, and notes of highlights from his readings in classic books by Andrew Murray, Hudson Taylor, Oswald Chambers, and others. He was a fountain of praise as he spoke of God's goodness, wisdom, and faithfulness. His faith was nourished through a continual feast of spiritual truth and prayer time, and he encouraged others with his indomitable spirit. When he felt worse, his inspirational reaction was, "Praise the Lord, it only means that I am one day closer to my day of healing."

I was teaching elementary school during the day, taking time off for the necessary medical appointments and travel. My best times were those in which I could find a quiet spot to read, read, read, and pray, pray, pray. God's Word was my sustenance. Together, Pat and I had opportunities to talk to friends and strangers about our journey of faith. Pat boldly expressed his faith to the doctors and nurses who saw him. He spoke about his relationship with Jesus, and the inner strength and peace he felt even though his physical prognosis was unfavorable. He was clear about not being afraid to die. People told us they could see real peace on our faces, and they wanted to know how that could be. It was a joy to tell them it was because of Jesus, and we were blessed to pray with some of them as they received Jesus as their Savior.

Where was the victory? We expected the victory to come in a tidy little box labeled, "Healed." Instead, it came in a huge, lumpy package labeled, "Perseverance, Faith, Praise, Peace, Trust, and Souls for Heaven." Am I thrilled to have experienced those victories? Yes, I am. But did I wrestle with it after Pat died? Yes, I did. I wondered if I could hear from God. How could I have missed what He was saying to us? *Did* I miss it? Or was there something more I needed to understand from Him that some day would come into focus? Yes, there was more to understand.

Victory encompasses a more lasting experience than the production of a miracle, however great that single event might be. Victory wraps around everything we are. We are clothed in victory, Christ's victory. Because of this, victory is displayed every day when we walk by faith, especially when we bow to the sovereign will and wisdom of our God, giving up our right to receive a particular answer to a particular prayer. God is glorified by unconditional faith; I cannot establish boundaries, terms of agreement, or conditions in my relationship with God. The Old Testament story of Shadrach, Meshach and Abednego is an inspiring demonstration of such lavish faith. Faced with the choice of bowing down to King Nebuchadnezzar's idol-gods, or remaining true to their God— in which case they would be thrown into the king's furnace— they boldly stated their unwavering commitment to the one true God:

> *"O Nebuchadnezzar, we do not need to give you an answer concerning this matter. If it be so, our God whom we serve is able to deliver us from the furnace of blazing fire; and He will deliver us out of your hand, O king.*
>
> ***"But even if He does not,*** *let it be known to you, O king, that we are not going to serve your gods or worship the golden image that you have set up"* (Daniel 3:16-18).

They stated they knew their God was able to deliver them from the fire, but being delivered was not their priority. Their priority was to be loyal servants of their God, the God of

Abraham, Isaac, and Jacob. And God saw them through their literal fiery trial. He was with them in the fire (Daniel 3:19), and delivered them out of their expected destruction. The three men had been willing to accept death rather than deny their allegiance to their God. The Lord was pleased to see such faith and to show His mighty power in return.

Brian, Kathi, Etta, and I spoke at Pat's memorial service. Brian and Kathi each wrote moving words about their father. Etta told stories about special times she had spent with him when he walked out his faith. I wanted everyone to know that although I was shocked and desperately grieving his death, I felt blessed to have been given faith to live the last two years knowing God would work everything out in His perfect way. But I also felt it was important to be honest about my questions. After thanking the gathered friends and family for their outpourings of love, encouragement, and prayers, I said,

"I'm like you—I have more questions than answers today. But this I know: that certainly, without a doubt: faith has not failed, prayer has not failed, nor has God failed us. God *never* fails.

"We have struggled in the last four days to understand this course of events that actually caught many of us by surprise—for there were those of us, including Pat, who prayed and believed that God would bring him complete healing, for the purpose of glorifying the name of Jesus Christ, his Savior. Pat's passion was that a growing number of people would be encouraged to believe God's promises as they are recorded in the Bible, and would discover the peace, joy, love, and faith that comes from living in harmony with God's Word. So many times I heard Pat say, 'It doesn't matter how things look, my eyes are on the Living God who controls all things. And God never makes mistakes.'

"Pat talked about God's reality being a greater reality than that of this earth. What he spoke of, he saw with the eyes of faith; and although he did not expect it to come so soon, he looked forward to the life that he is now experiencing. This is truly our loss, but is just as truly Pat's gain. Pat recently told me of a vivid picture that came to his mind. He said, 'I saw myself just running and running, with my arms high in the air, praising God.' I can easily envision him, even now, doing just that.

"I have wondered so much in the last four days why I should have felt so absolutely confident that Pat would be healed on earth, when that turned out not to be the case. And although I don't know the complete answer to that, we didn't lose a thing by believing God would work a miracle. After all, we've seen miracles before—some of them are in this room right now! The Bible describes God as the God of all hope, and God of the impossible, and the One who forms our futures with His loving hands. How terrible it would have been, had we lived the last two years in fear and despair, without hope. God gave us two years of love, joy, peace, and faith, while we trusted in His wisdom and loving intervention for us. Pat and I planned for the days that would follow his healing.

"I don't regret a single bit of that. It was joyous—because it wasn't just wishful thinking to be making future plans. It was based on our experience that God is great, and nothing is too hard for Him to do, and that when people pray, and when faith is linked to God's Word, amazing, even miraculous, things may happen. That faith kept us, and I would choose the same attitude of faith again. The Bible says, *'Now the God of hope fill you with all joy and peace in believing, that ye may abound in hope'* (Romans 15:13).

"It's not a bad way to live. Because 'Remember,' Pat would say, 'God doesn't make mistakes.' Pat's faith in Jesus Christ, his love for God, and his heart for prayer are treasures he shared with us. May those beautiful treasures be multiplied."

Heaven will reveal the treasures that were stored up by those who walked in faith, trusting God beyond human logic and visible evidences. And the treasures left behind by a godly life as inspiration for others will one day be gathered up and added to the storehouse in heaven.

There is an awesome peace that settles into the soul when I realize God's definition of victory is broader than mine and more lasting—in fact, it is eternally significant. One of the Bible verses Pat recorded in his journal of favorite words and songs is from 2 Corinthians.

"All this is for your benefit, so that the grace that is reaching more and more people may cause thanksgiving to overflow to the glory of God. Therefore we do not lose heart. Though outwardly we are wasting away, yet inwardly we are being renewed day by day. For our light and momentary troubles are achieving for us an eternal glory that far outweighs them all" (2 Corinthians 4:15-17). (ASV)

It is difficult to remember that I am on this earth only temporarily and that my true home is in heaven. But when I redirect my thoughts to this and refresh my perceptions, the disjointed fragments of life's trials and triumphs begin to fit together comfortably for the first time. I struggle much with my limited view of events and their significance. Everything is colored by my personal desires and experiences. It's nearly impossible to avoid those biases. It takes mental discipline and the help of the Holy Spirit to set aside my human viewpoint in order to achieve an eternal perspective on my losses, disappointments, and pain.

The only way I can effectively refocus my thoughts and get a new perspective is to be transformed through the Word of God. Sometimes after reading a Scripture that speaks to my immediate need, I stop in awe, basking in the marvel of such a treasure. I read and contemplate recorded events, miracles, and God's instructions to His people. I read the words of Jesus as they are recorded in the gospels, and become familiar with the practical applications I need to make. All these experiences in the Bible work in my mind and change my viewpoint to more closely reflect God's way of thinking about things. Truly His Word is *"like a lamp unto my feet and a light unto my path."* We rarely can see the whole path, but we are given enough light for the next step. This is the victory—when by faith we take the next step! I know when I've I reached that place of new perspective because the darkness that felt like it was hovering over me evaporates, and it is like coming into a beautiful sun-soaked meadow.

There are many lessons to learn while we're on this path of faith. Our journey is with a Faithful Companion, and the destination and rewards are worth every struggle. One day the challenges will be forgotten when the victorious celebrations begin. I've already begun to celebrate. I may not be out of the woods yet, but there are fewer trees.

❈❈❈

"I have come that they might have life, and that they might have it more abundantly." (John 10:10 KJV)

Notes

(Italics added; not in original works)

PREFACE: "How Do You Get That Kind of Faith?"

[1] Tree of knowledge of good and evil—"but *you must not eat from the tree of the knowledge of good and evil,* for when you eat from it you will certainly die" (Genesis 2:9).

[2] Temptation of the devil— "Now the serpent was more crafty than any beast of the field which the Lord God had made. And he said to the woman, "Indeed, has God said, 'You shall not eat from any tree of the garden'?…and *she took from its fruit* and ate; and she gave it *also to her husband with her,* and he ate" (Genesis 3:1-6).

[3] Every person is now tainted by original sin— "…for *all have sinned* and fall short of the glory of God" (Romans 3:23).

[4] Jesus took on human form and is sinless— 2 Corinthians 5:21 "God made him *who had no sin* to be sin for us, so that in him we might become the righteousness of God" (NIV).

[5] Jesus was God on earth— "Behold the virgin will be with child and shall bear a son and shall call His name Immanuel," which translated means, *"GOD WITH US."* (Matthew 1:23 KJV).

[6] Punishment for sins of the world— "We have seen and testify that the Father has sent the Son to be the *Savior of the world*" 1 John 4:14). Also, "The next day he saw Jesus coming to him and said, "Behold, the Lamb of God who takes away the *sin of the world*" (John 1:29).

⁷ Nailed offenses weren't His— "...having canceled out the certificate of debt consisting of *decrees against us*, which was hostile to us; and He has taken it out of the way, having nailed it to the cross" (Colossians 2:14).

⁸ Cross gives us forgiveness from God— "In him we have redemption *through his blood*, the *forgiveness of sins,* in accordance with the riches of God's grace" (Ephesians 1:7. NIV). "...Remember that you were at that time separate from Christ ... having no hope and without God in the world. But now in Christ Jesus you who formerly were far off have been *brought near by the blood of Christ*" (Ephesians 2:12-14).

⁹ We are made acceptable to God, fit for heaven— "Yet to all who did receive him, to those who believed in his name, he *gave the right to become children of God*" John 1:12). Also, "...and giving joyful thanks to the Father, who has *qualified you to share in the inheritance of his holy people* in the kingdom of light. For he has rescued us from the dominion of darkness and brought us *into the kingdom* of the Son he loves" (Colossians 1:12-13 NIV).

¹⁰ Abundant life—"I came that they may *have life and have it abundantly*" (John 10:10).

¹¹"I am the Way, the Truth and the Life"— "Jesus answered, '*I am the way and the truth and the life*. No one comes to the Father except through me'" (John 14:6 NIV).

¹² Faith like a mustard seed—"He replied, 'Because you have so little faith. Truly I tell you, if you have *faith as small as a mustard seed*, you can say to this mountain, 'Move from here to there,' and it will move. Nothing will be impossible for you'" (Matthew 17:20 NIV).

[13] Heaven forever, eternal life— "Jesus answered, 'The work of God is this: to believe in the one He has sent'" (John 6:29 NIV). "For this is the will of My Father, that everyone who beholds the Son and believes in Him *will have eternal life*, and I Myself will raise him up on the last day" (John 6:40).

CHAPTER 8: What is Faith, Anyway?

[1] Hayford, Jack. *Spirit-Formed*, The Angels are Still Singing, Part 2, broadcast Jan 2, 2011.

CHAPTER 11: More Precious than Gold

[1] Wuest, Kenneth. The New Testament: An Expanded Translation. Wm B. Eerdsman Publishing Co., 1961. p. 533-534.

CHAPTER 12: Joy and Peace in Believing

[1] Wuest, Kenneth. *Hebrews in the Greek New Testament.* Wuest's Word Studies from the Greek New Testament, Vol. Two. Wm. B. Eerdmans Publishing Company, Grand Rapids, Michigan.1973, reprinted 1995. p.536.

[2] Ibid., p.531.

[3] Ibid., p.533.

❧ Recommended Reading ❧

ESTELLE
by James W. Tharp

Estelle, a young woman in an isolated Arkansas county, longs to know God in a more personal way. Surrounded by intimidating characters and frightening events, Estelle's heart seeks refuge in prayer and in her discovery of a powerful and loving God. Against the odds of poverty, pride, and the provocations of a skeptical husband, Estelle discovers the secrets of prayer, surrender, and obedience to God, releasing the presence and power of the Holy Spirit in a way that transforms her husband, her family, and an entire community.

Many of the amazing events in this narrative actually happened, and are testimony to the love of a powerful, yet personal, God who hears the prayers of His children, meets urgent needs, and answers in miraculous ways in the most difficult of times.

The story of ESTELLE reminds us that no darkness is beyond the reach of prayer. The remarkable experiences of ESTELLE will astonish you and inspire you to experience the love of God in a greater way, increase your dependence on prayer, and deepen your own relationship with Jesus Christ.

In the **Grip** *of His Hand*
by Ruth Knoblock

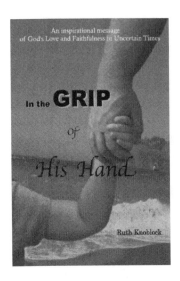

A book of encouragement and help for those wondering about the unexpected and unwelcome challenges that come in life. A collection of some of the author's extraordinary experiences and her insight into their important life lessons, these unusual and sometimes miraculous encounters prove God's great love shows up on a personal level. The stormy seas and rocky trails are not meant to destroy us, but to make us strong. We are invited to draw closer to the One who lovingly guides and faithfully provides, no matter how great the challenge. This edition has pages for the reader to journal their own thoughts and study notes.

Pieces of My Heart
by David L. Wood

David Wood's writing is a wonderful mixture of humor, insight, inspiration, and story-telling. Each chapter is short, perfect for a devotional daily reading, and worth reading in small doses in order to absorb all that is offered in just a few pages at a time. This is the kind of book you like to take on a trip, or keep handy at home for a quick read to inspire positive thoughts. You will enjoy the authenticity of the author, his stories, and the thoughtful applications for life's ups and downs. The author says, "Stories of great lessons are found all around us in our normal everyday lives if we will dare to open our eyes and see."

Made in the USA
Charleston, SC
11 July 2012